Work in the Balance

Vicky Cattell • Stephen Stansfeld

Work in the Balance

Influences on the Mental Health and Well-Being of Civil Servants

palgrave
macmillan

Vicky Cattell
Sociologist and formerly Honorary Senior Lecturer at the Centre for Psychiatry and Mental Health
Queen Mary, University of London
London, UK

Stephen Stansfeld
Emeritus Professor of Psychiatry at the Centre for Psychiatry and Mental Health, Barts and the London School of Medicine and Dentistry
Queen Mary, University of London
London, UK

ISBN 978-3-031-96581-4 ISBN 978-3-031-96582-1 (eBook)
https://doi.org/10.1007/978-3-031-96582-1

This Palgrave Macmillan imprint is published by the registered company Springer Nature Switzerland AG.
The registered company address is: Gewerbestrasse 11, 6330 Cham, Switzerland

Foreword

The Whitehall II study set out to examine the role of psychosocial influences in health and health inequalities. The unstated assumption was that the material problems of life, and associated ill-health, had been 'solved' in contemporary Britain. Causes of ill-health were likely to act through the mind, influencing behaviour and stress pathways.

The second part is correct; causes of ill-health *are* likely to act through the mind. But the material problems of life have not been 'solved'. For example, with Friends of the Earth the Institute of Health Equity, in February 2024, released a report on cold homes, 'Left Out in the Cold'. We reported that, in the UK, 9.6 million households, a third of the total, can't afford a decent standard of living and are in poorly insulated homes that are expensive to heat. Living in a cold home will damage physical and mental health of children and adults.

Along the same lines, in late 2023, the Joseph Rowntree Foundation published their report into Destitution in the UK. Destitution was defined as doing without two or more of six essentials: housing, heat, light, food, clothing, toiletries. In 2022, 3.8 million people, 1 million of whom were children, were in a state of destitution. Health will suffer as a result.

This book is a welcome reminder that we need to be focussed on material needs, of course, but psychological and social needs are of vital importance, too. I do not take the view of a hierarchy of needs. We need to deal with physical essentials and social and psychological needs at the same time.

This qualitative study of the lives of civil servants illustrates the many reasons why people go to work. One basic reason is money. As I write this, one man in his ninth decade is competing with another only four years younger to be the next President of the United States. They are not doing it for the money, although the younger man may be doing it because the White House is preferable to prison. Work provides other rewards—personal fulfilment, respect from others, satisfaction at making a contribution, social relationships, a social role. We tried to capture these different aspects in our quantitative studies of psychosocial influences on mental and physical illness in the Whitehall II study of British civil servants. The success of these efforts was shown in the results on the effects on health of stress in the workplace.

A qualitative study such as this present one provides nuance and insight beyond that available in our epidemiological research. It is worth keeping these nuances in mind when listening to what the government has in mind for the public sector. In the March 2024 Budget [prior to the change of Government in July], the British Chancellor (finance minister) cut national insurance payments—essentially a tax cut—thus reducing the revenue that the government receives. These cuts notionally are to be paid for by 'efficiencies' in the public sector. Assuming for the moment that these 'efficiencies' are not phantasies, one wonders what the government has in mind.

Reading the experiences reported here, it is highly likely that efficiencies would make everyone's experiences at work a good deal worse. The higher grade civil servants appreciate the importance and variety of the work, but not when they feel out of control. Efficiencies, essentially cuts, foisted on them without adequate thought and planning are likely to reduce agency and associated job satisfaction. Increased risk of ill-health will be the result.

The lower grades appear not to gain much satisfaction from routine work tasks, but gain a great deal from their social relations in the workplace. What would cuts do to that? The middle grades appreciated the work-life balance. That, too, would be a casualty of thoughtless 'efficiency savings'.

The importance of this study is the rich understanding it conveys of the different life experiences of people at different levels of the social hierarchy in British society. The lives of low grade civil servants are more restricted than those above them in the hierarchy, partly a result of less education and lower incomes, but also the nature of the work. Routine office-based tasks will always be less interesting than that of higher grade civil servants. But surely it is possible to design work in such a way that it is life enhancing not something that would harm health were it not for the presence of social supports. Given that such supports are necessary, work should be designed to foster those, too.

Such hierarchies at work are unlikely to be confined to the public sector. But, it is the case, that the public sector has been devalued by successive governments as part of their lack of regard for the public good. The British economy as a whole has been marked by lack of improvement in productivity, worse than in other rich countries. Improvements are needed. They will not be achieved by foisting cuts, in the name of productivity, on the public sector. The insight of this study is that great damage may be done.

To improve health and reduce health inequalities society needs to address the material disadvantages that still scar Britain today and lead to a shameful toll of preventable ill-health. We need more: living and working conditions that meet the needs mentioned above—self-fulfilment, respect, social purpose, good social relations. The present study provides us with just the kind of insight that is necessary to inform the arrangements of work and society necessary for better health and narrower health inequalities. The gains could not be more important: improvements in the conditions in which people live and work, giving people the conditions under which to fashion lives of meaning, purpose, and satisfaction.

Department for Epidemiology & Public Health, Institute of Health Equity, University College London, London, UK
2024

Sir Michael Marmot

Ethics Approval

Ethical approval for the Whitehall II study was obtained from the University College London Medical School committee on the effects of human research. Ethical guidelines produced by academic and professional bodies such as the Social Research Association and the British Sociological Association were also consulted.

Acknowledgements

This work has been supported by a grant from the ESRC *Health Variations Programme*, Phase II (L128251052).

We are indebted to Professor Sir Michael Marmot leader of the Whitehall II Stress and Health studies, and to the Whitehall II team for enabling access to the Whitehall II data base. Our thanks are due to Jenny Head, who conducted the sampling procedure, to Rebecca Fuhrer for her contribution to the early phase of the work, and to the civil servants who kindly gave of their time and shared their thoughts and experiences with us.

Competing Interests The authors have no competing interests to declare that are relevant to the content of this manuscript.

Contents

CHAPTER 1

Introduction

Abstract Discussion on the role of work for the twenty-first century has focused on both benefits and harmful effects of the working environment. The Whitehall II Stress and Health studies have shown the many disbenefits of employment to be unevenly distributed between social groups. Yet we suspected that the quantitative differences identified in these studies may not provide the whole picture, the effects of pathways linking features such as work characteristics and material factors to common mental disorders or to positive aspects of well-being could be expected to be conveyed through the meaning of stressors for example, or mediated through individual perceptions of work. Based on a qualitative research project, this book examines and illustrates ways in which a wide range of stressors, mitigators, and resources are not only socially distributed and experienced but also interpreted and understood by men and women in different civil service grades. Adopting a holistic and sociological approach to the research helps us to understand why some people and not others in given circumstances feel out of control or become anxious or depressed.

Keywords Work • Civil servants • Stress • Depression • Meanings • Orientations • Work characteristics • Insecurity • inequalities • Qualitative

V. Cattell, S. Stansfeld, *Work in the Balance*,
https://doi.org/10.1007/978-3-031-96582-1_1

The role and value of work for the twenty-first century has become a prominent focus of interest. Some of the issues raised are especially apposite for a post pandemic world and a society in which we face increasingly precarious employment, a fragmented workforce, and less steady career progression (see, e.g., Sennett, 1998; Castells, 1996). Findlay and Thompson (2017), in mapping the changing nature of employment, have highlighted issues around insecurity, increased demands, performance management, problems concerning work/life balance, and engagement or disengagement with work. Gaillie et al. (2017) argue that while research on job insecurity has focused on job loss, status insecurity, which they define as valued features of the job, has been neglected.

Questions are now being asked about whether we need work (Taylor, 2021), whether technological advances will render much work unnecessary (Cruddas, 2021; Mason, 2016; Skidelsky & Glassman, 2013), about the role of A.I., and about the desirability of a society in which our lives no longer revolve around the drudgery and loss of autonomy associated with work (Srnicek & Williams, 2015). Whether a world without work is something to fear or to welcome as liberating from unsatisfying tasks, the future of work, as Michael Sandel (2018b) recognises, is something we, and political parties, will have to get to grips with along with the *meaning* of work and its place in a good life. A 'good life', for the purposes of our own research, would be one at low risk from mental illness and poor well-being.

As well as an improved income, the potentially positive benefits to health of being in work as opposed to experiencing unemployment—such as the opportunities work offers to develop skills, gain self-esteem, recognition, self-respect, identity, dignity, belonging, status, and integration, to pursue regular activity and bestow a sense of purpose and meaning to our lives—are many (Bolton & Laaser, 2013; Budd, 2011; Cruddas, 2021; Jahoda, 1982; Mandemakers & Monden, 2013; Siegrist, 1996). Nonetheless, official statistics and academic research demonstrate that the work environment can also harm us. Health and Safety Executive figures show an increase in work-related stress, anxiety, and depression in recent years: these accounted for 51% of all work-related ill health cases in the year 2019/20. Mental ill health is more prevalent in certain sectors, public administration—the focus of our study—included (Health and Safety Executive, 2020). Work can negatively affect people's lives through, for example, a spill-over of work responsibilities into home time, through encountering discrimination, by producing feelings of insecurity, or upsetting work/life balance (Bhui et al., 2005; Ferrie et al., 2003; McNamara et al., 2013; Schnall et al., 2009; Stansfeld et al., 2004).

Work Characteristics

Especially detrimental effects involve the impact on mental health and well-being of certain work characteristics, and which can be experienced as feelings of stress. Prolonged stress can result in anxiety, burnout, and depression (see, e.g., Dobson & Schnall, 2009). Burnout, a less familiar term than depression or anxiety perhaps, has been defined as emotional exhaustion, cynicism (negative feelings about work and distancing from others), and a lack of accomplishment (Dobson & Schnall, 2009). Work characteristics which have been shown to increase the risk of common mental disorders (anxiety and depression) include such features as job strain, effort/reward imbalance, high work demands, long working hours, intensification, shift work, bullying, organisational injustice, management style, racial discrimination, and job insecurity (Boxall & Macky, 2014; Ferrie et al., 2003; Gordon & Schnall, 2009; Stansfeld & Candy, 2006). Respondents to a Health and Safety Executive survey identified workload pressure involving tight deadlines, too much responsibility, and a lack of managerial support (HSE, 2020) as particularly damaging influences on work-related stress, depression, or anxiety. A quite shocking example of the effects of post-Taylorism and Scientific Management adopted in the public sector, found that 'lean' working, that is, a focus on narrow, single tasks, along with lack of control of the work process, contributed to mental fatigue, stress, and headaches amongst clerical workers exposed to it (Carter et al., 2013). Some of the strongest epidemiological evidence relates to features of the work task and ways in which work is organised: low decision authority/latitude (or job control); high job demands (work pace and conflicting demands); and a perceived effort/reward imbalance, for example (Siegrist, 1996). Job strain occurs when high demands are combined with low control (Karasek & Theorell, 1990; Stansfeld & Candy, 2006). Work characteristics like these have been shown to predict psychiatric disorder (Stansfeld et al., 1999).

Changes in the working environment in recent decades include many considered to have a largely detrimental effect on the quality of jobs and the well-being of those in work (Carter et al., 2013). Researchers have described work as being in a state of 'crisis'. Contemporary forms of work, it is argued, create problems for human capabilities and well-being

(Strangleman, 2012; Weeks, 2011). A growth in work intensification processes is frequently identified as a major culprit. Intensification is a form of work associated with fatigue, stress, and a rupture of work/life balance (Boxall & Macky, 2014; Carter et al., 2013; Warhurst et al., 2012).

Satisfaction with Work

A separate though related body of research has explored the influences on and effects of job satisfaction and dissatisfaction. Attention has been given for example to the relative importance of intrinsic (features of the work itself), or extrinsic (such as remuneration and terms of contract) rewards, and their contribution to job satisfaction (Zou, 2015). Gallie's work, following Maslow (1954), who identified a hierarchy of needs, has suggested that those with higher rates of pay attach more importance to intrinsic features of work (Gaillie et al., 2012). The literature provides some conflicting evidence, however. Rose (2003) enumerates the many sharp inequalities which exist between occupations in levels of remuneration, contract of employment, career opportunities and status, as well as time pressures, stress levels, influence over work assignments, opportunities for initiative, power in the workplace, and interest content of the job (Rose, 2003). While varying levels of job satisfaction are found between occupations in the UK, Rose also found however that these inequalities do not necessarily follow standard measures of social stratification closely.

Social Inequality

Nonetheless, the many benefits and disbenefits of employment have been shown to be unevenly distributed between social groups, and, as Savage et al. (2015) suggests, inequality is the defining issue of our time. The Whitehall II Stress and Health studies have made a major contribution to our knowledge of the structuring of social inequalities in physical and mental health (Marmot, 2020; Marmot et al., 1991) and have identified many of the risk factors involved (Marmot et al., 1997; Stansfeld et al., 1998). Features such as work characteristics, social support, and life events affect health and vary by employment grade. As part of the ESRC *Health Variations Programme*, the qualitative research project on which this book is based examined the contribution of work-based factors to the explanation of the social class gradient in mental health and well-being. Earlier work established statistical associations between work characteristics such as control over work and skill discretion, and the grade gradient in depression (Stansfeld et al., 1998). Just as stressors are differentiated by class and gender, resources—both material (e.g., income and housing) and psychosocial (e.g., control at work)—vary by socio-economic status (Marmot et al., 1991). Yet we suspected that the quantitative differences identified in Whitehall II studies may not provide the whole picture, whilst illustrative of general trends, statistics can explain little of how they happen (Popay et al., 1998). The effects of pathways linking features such as work characteristics and material factors like income or educational level to common mental disorders (Muntaner et al., 2004; Stansfeld & Candy, 2006) or to positive aspects of well-being could be expected to be conveyed through the *meaning* of stressors, for example, or mediated through individual perceptions of work or to aspects of individual agency. It would be difficult, for example, to separate work-related susceptibility to psychiatric disorder from how the person perceives, interacts with, and reacts to working conditions, colleagues, and supervisors. We thought it likely that there may be different as well as similar interpretations of and reactions to the working environment according to employment grade. The chapters which follow consider and illustrate ways in which a wide range of stressors and resources are socially distributed, experienced, and interpreted by people in different civil service grades and examine their contribution to social inequalities in mental health and well-being.

A Holistic Approach

Exploration of a wide range of stressors and mitigators requires a holistic approach to researching people's lives. One of the objectives of the study was to explore the explanatory value of the stress hypothesis—in which ill-health results from an imbalance of demands over resources—in understanding relationships between psychosocial factors and mental ill-health (see, e.g., Dobson & Schnall, 2009). Stressors (risk factors) derive from many and diverse aspects of experience: life events like bereavement, job loss or moving home; chronic difficulties, such as poverty, long standing illness, poor housing, depleted local facilities and resources, fear of crime or racial assault, as well as social isolation, negative interactions in close relationships and, in the workplace, high job demands and low job control. Factors such as social support at home or work, high levels of control over work, and skill discretion can be protective or act as more direct resources. People with lower levels of education have fewer economic and social resources to help avoid stressful events and to successfully cope with them (Miech & Shanahan, 2000; Turner et al., 1995).

Pearlin has suggested that understanding stress requires a holistic approach involving exploration of structure, context, complexity, and process (Pearlin, 1989) elements which are the focus of qualitative approaches. The social structures Pearlin identifies range from stratification and economic structure through to social institutions—work or family—and interpersonal relationships, as well as contextual influences such as place of residence. The complexities of the stress process involve stressors, mediators, and stress outcomes. The likely contagion and precipitation of stressors derived from different areas of one's life, means that research studies must cast a wide net to capture the full array of stressors in an individual's life, as well as the values which help shape their meaning (Pearlin, 1989). A wide research net, we conjecture, is also necessary if we are to capture a full range of supports and other coping or direct resources available. A holistic perspective is considered appropriate for employment related as well as health focused research: the adoption of a research framework which could capture both the rich and the impoverished nature of employment and social relationships in and out of organisations has been advocated for example (Bolton & Laaser, 2013). Taking a contextual approach, social scientists emphasise the need to explore conditions under which stressors will and will not have an influence on psychological functioning. Consideration is encouraged of the broader circumstances that may create, suppress, or accentuate the association between, for example, socioeconomic position (SEP) and stress; the explanatory mechanisms involved may differ across contexts (Miech & Shanahan, 2000; Montez & Friedman, 2015).

The multifarious influences on depression and other common mental disorders evident from the research literature underline the desirability for research imperatives to reach beyond the individual's position in, and experience of the workplace and work task: we include civil servants' experience of and perceptions of life outside work as additional foci of interest in this study. Work, perhaps for women more than men, will be only one of many roles undertaken (Stansfeld et al., 2004). Perceptions of neighbourhood have been shown to be important influences on mental health for instance (Ziersch et al., 2004), and studies have shown that place based communities still have relevance in people's lives, for meeting needs for belonging and identity for example, for developing supportive social networks, and for their health and well-being (Mulligan, 2015; Cattell &

Herring, 2002a; Cattell & Herring, 2002b; Cattell & Evans, 1999; Cattell, 2003; Cattell, 2012; Elliott et al., 2014). A holistic perspective sits comfortably with 'well-being' explorations as well as more conventional psychiatric measures of mental ill health. Sayer (2011), while recognising well-being as a complex construction, places emphasis on the ability to develop and exercise our capacities across different contexts.

Well-being

Quantitative research findings briefly introduced above demonstrate well established relationships between conventional measures of mental health and work characteristics and social support. Less work, however, has been undertaken (in epidemiology at least) in which the focus is on subjective measures of well-being. Exceptions include work which, using the Bradburn Affect Balance scale—a measure of social psychological well-being—found that high levels of control at work, low levels of job strain, and high levels of personal social support were associated with higher levels of well-being (Stansfeld et al., 2013).

Commonly used definitions of well-being feature subjective perceptions of moods such as happiness and judgement of life satisfaction (Ryan & Deci, 2001), having control over one's life and a sense of purpose as well as functioning effectively. Enthusiasm for life and being actively engaged with others (Keyes, 2002) also come into the frame, as do, more simply put, lives going well, that is, eudaimonic well-being (Huppert, 2009). Some contemporary approaches define the concept with regard to the satisfaction of human social and emotional needs, and needs for self-actualisation (Pickering, 2001); they can refer also to material wants, aesthetic pleasure (Gesler, 2003) or a sense of belonging or identity, and feeling comfortable with one's world (Dupois & Thorns, 1998). Critics of aspects of the 'human flourishing' approach to well-being and happiness which regard the individual self and its needs as the central focus of concern, argue that traditionally held virtues such as hard work, sacrifice, altruism, and commitment have become devalued (Cieslik, 2015; Furedi, 2004; Pahl, 1995). For Layard happiness is a balance between good and bad experience, and is not simply about pleasure. We should be wary, in any case, that happiness agendas may be in danger of sidelining the significance of the benefits of certain material factors on well-being.

There are however real advantages in utilising concepts of well-being in research. The World Health Organization's interpretation of 'well-being' as 'positive health' (WHO, 1948), for example, a state of complete physical, mental, and social well-being and not merely the absence of disease or infirmity (WHO, 1948), enables a focus on what promotes and protects health, rather than on what causes illness. It is understood by sociologists as a dimension of a 'social model' of health which locates individual experience within social contexts and is concerned especially with people's interpretation of them (Gatrell et al., 2000). While research on work-related stress tends to focus on the negative consequences of work, a positive health perspective provides opportunities to examine factors which improve the work environment and its health related benefits. The WHO treats *positive* mental health holistically, delineating it as 'a state of well-being in which the individual realises his or her own abilities, can cope with the normal stresses of life, can work productively and fruitfully, and is able to make a contribution to his or her community' (WHO, 2001, 2018). Work influenced by the WHO's perspective considered local communities for example as potential sites for the nurturance of positive well-being (Cattell, 2012), whilst the adoption of a holistic approach to researching mental health and well-being is supported by research which has noted that people speak about deriving a sense of well-being and happiness from diverse sources and from different domains of their lives (Cattell & Herring, 2002a; Cattell & Herring, 2002b; Cieslik, 2015; Pahl, 1995).

Social Ties

While perspectives of well-being are seemingly diverse, they most typically embrace social dimensions including the quality of social relationships (Haidt, 2006; Keyes, 2002; Layard, 2011). Marx (1844) understood the antithesis of well-being as alienation, that is, separation from others, from our social being, and dislocation from our species being, our true selves, as well as the more familiar separation from our labour and the product of our work. Lack of social support is acknowledged as a contributory factor to depression, but, rather surprisingly, a Whitehall II study found personal social support not to be a powerful explanation of grade differences in depressive symptoms (Stansfeld et al., 2003). Reconciling anomalous and contradictory findings on social support evident in Whitehall II studies and seeking analytical purchase on processes involved in relationships between support and mental health and well-being might necessitate taking a considered approach to social ties which includes a focus on such factors as their importance and meaning to the individual, or which ventures beyond their role in the provision of support. Not all social relationships are experienced as positive, they can sometimes be perceived as oppressive by those receiving support, or as burdensome by those providing it (Crow, 2004), or may have a malign influence on health related behaviour (Kirke, 2006; Kunitz, 2001). Nevertheless, in most circumstances, being part of an extensive social network is beneficial to the health of individuals across social groups (Blaxter, 1990; Kawachi & Berkman, 2001; Valente, 2010). Social ties are seen as acting either as a buffer against stressful life events and a protection against depression, or as exerting a more direct influence (Brown & Harris, 1978). Social support—practical, instrumental, or emotional aid—has been consistently shown to have a positive influence on health and well-being (Cohen & Syme, 1985; Hildon et al., 2008; Stansfeld et al., 1999; Whelan, 1993). More generally, studies have shown that social networks, as well as providing opportunities for companionship and sociability, have the capacity to confer social esteem or a feeling of belonging, or contribute to positive self-identity and a sense of coherence (Allan, 1996; Antonovsky, 1987; Cattell, 2004; Wellman & Wortley, 1990). A classic workplace study indicated that strong work-based social networks can be a source of greater worker control and empowerment (Blauner, 1964). Earlier work based on interviews with people living in low-income areas argued that social networks are significant mediators and key moderators between the harsh circumstances of people's lives and their lived experience of health and well-being (Cattell, 2004; Cattell, 2012).

Meanings Attached to Work

In this study we expected the meanings individuals attach to work and to their local environment to play an important role in mental health and well-being outcomes. Amongst the particular approaches taken is the consideration of work as a positive value, as a source of satisfaction, for example, as well as a potential stressor. A seminal social study on attitudes and behaviour in the workplace (Goldthorpe et al., 1968), argued that the satisfactions people gain from work must be considered in relation to *orientations* to work, to the variety of meanings that work has for employees. Although based on a study of workers in industry, their perspective nevertheless provides an appropriate starting point for analysing research into the lives of public sector employees. For example, when referring to researchers in the human relations school (Mayo, 1949) who proposed that people seek needs of a social kind from work—acceptance, approval, recognition, etc.—and that where these 'higher level' needs are not met, suffer psychologically, Goldthorpe and Lockwood argue instead that our wants and expectations are not constants but culturally and socially determined, and suggest that orientations may be intelligible in relation to their social correlates, and to individuals' roles outside work, such as those taking place in family or community contexts, as well as in work (Goldthorpe et al., 1968). The present study looks at variation in meanings and their sources and considers to what extent and in what ways meanings moderate work characteristics and mental health and well-being.

Taking a wider ranging approach to the meanings of work, as we noted at the beginning of this chapter, while some theorists look to utopian notions of a workless future (Skidelsky & Glassman, 2013; Vogt, 2016) an alternative approach elevates work as central to our lives, giving us meaning and fulfilment—a good in its own right (Breen, 2007). Work can give us a common understanding of a shared humanity; work matters to us not only individually, but collectively, as humans (Biggs, 2015; Lucassen, 2021). For Andrew Sayer (2009) 'our work has a major influence on our character, capacities, and hence our well-being'. He argues that the character and quality of work shapes the worker's self-development and can provide fulfilment, respect, and self-esteem. Work can promise a great deal therefore, but how do we reconcile understandings like this with suffering, with the reality of the many detrimental effects on mental health and well-being associated with aspects of work? Inequalities in the availability of meaningful work (Gomberg, 2007; Sayer, 2009) must be considered.

Study Aims

We anticipated that a qualitative study would throw some further light on unresolved issues involved in the relationship between stressors (features such as work demands), mediators and moderators (such as meanings and support), and pathways (like control and esteem), and mental health and well-being

The primary aims of the study were to:

- Uncover a variety of meanings which people attach to their employment and to the characteristics of the work they experience and to take note of social variation.

- Consider the extent to which the health effects of difficulties at work are contingent on the different meanings and values invested in those perceptions.
- Throw further light on pathways involved in social inequalities in mental health and well-being and on unresolved issues involved in the relationship between stressors (features such as work demands), mediators and moderators (such as meanings and support), and pathways (like control and esteem), and mental health and positive well-being.
- Address anomalous and contradictory findings on social support evident in Whitehall II studies and on findings that the impact of exposure to negative work characteristics on mental health is worse for lower grades.

We also approach work as a positive value, as a source of satisfaction, for example, as well as a potential stressor, and are mindful of the contribution played by wider aspects of individual's lives.

Research Methods

There are several potential advantages to adopting qualitative methodologies when seeking to advance our understanding of health inequalities in the workplace. They are suited to a perspective which seeks to embrace complexity and variability, can enable a focus on processes and mechanisms involved in health determinants and facilitate the retention of situations in their wider social and historical context. In-depth qualitative methods are particularly suited to approaches which view phenomena from the perspective of those being studied (Bulmer, 1984; Hammersley & Atkinson, 1995). Interactionist theory stressed the individual's subjective interpretation of a situation as key as well as the constraints which impinge on her or him. The familiar Thomas and Thomas aphorism that 'when men define situations as real, they are real in their consequences' (Thomas & Thomas, 1929, p. 572) exemplifies the point.

Seventy-six in-depth interviews with a sub sample of middle-aged civil servants were carried out, a demographic particularly relevant to the focus of this health study. Middle-aged people—those between 40 and 59 years of age—have been shown generally to have the highest levels of anxiety, and the lowest levels of life satisfaction and happiness compared to younger and older people (ONS, 2016). Additionally, a middle-aged group could show potential to gain insights which draw on many years of experience. Our sample was stratified by employment grade: Higher (Administrative), Middle (Executive), and Lower (Clerical/support), as well as gender and General Health Questionnaire (Goldberg & Hillier, 1979) anxiety and depression scores, low, medium, and high scores from the Whitehall II cohort. Civil Service employment grade, though not a replica of social class divisions, has been used in Whitehall II studies to provide a finely graded measure of occupational class position. It reflects levels of income and education, work responsibilities, and prestige. To capture wider aspects of deprivation than those associated with civil service grade, people living in rented accommodation were deliberately overrepresented, an appropriate strategy for studying this population as quantitative work undertaken as part of the larger study indicated that social gradients in depression were seen to be steeper in measures like financial difficulties and shallower with occupationally based measures of social position (Stansfeld et al., 2003). The sample was drawn from all London departments and, as well as people working in the Service, included a small minority who had taken early retirement or moved on to other jobs. These categories of informant were retained because of evident grade and gender variation in early retirement or new job move. Cohort statistics indicate for example that higher grades and men are overrepresented in both categories (Mein et al., 2000). Push and pull factors involved were also expected to be potentially interesting; it has been estimated for example that up to 40% of turnover in the workforce can be attributed to stressors at work, including lack of work-life balance, effort reward imbalance, and job strain (Jauregui & Schnall, 2009).

The interviews were set within the wider framework of respondents' everyday lives, in mundane lived experiences and routine interactions with others, and in different contexts; a common technique used in empirical sociological studies (Lechner, 1991; Neal & Murji, 2015). There have been calls for many more qualitative research projects on well-being that offer insights into the things that really matter to us as humans (Sayer, 2011). To address complexity, and both focus on individual cases and facilitate comparison with others, we used a flexible semi-structured interview schedule which, although including targeted questions, was nevertheless conversational and wide-ranging in scope. It looked at opportunities available to people and constraints which limit them, as well as at ways in which individuals perceive, interact, and react to their environment. We consider it important to look at how complex and reflexive relationships operate in given circumstances to affect mental health and well-being. Depression, for example, can be interpreted as a collapse of agency (Hoggett, 2001). The schedule focused on three specific contexts: work, neighbourhood, and home, with the greater emphasis on work. As Taylor (2021) argues, work is central to our lives and culture. Neighbourhood is included as an aid to exploring the wider picture in relation to both stressors and resources because its significance for processes involved in health and well-being may vary by grade and gender, and because it can enable a qualitative focus on looser, as well as stronger ties. Earlier work demonstrated the importance of both forms of ties to coping and well-being (Cattell, 2001). Respondents were also encouraged to reflect on their past as well as current lives. The interviews were conducted before the Covid pandemic, that is, before the abnormal working conditions—working from home especially—adopted in the public sector for the duration. Now that civil servants have returned to their more usual ways of working, the issues raised by our participants remain highly relevant for today.

Wider Topics Explored via the Questionnaire Included

Their neighbourhood, its sense of community, and local problems; everyday activities; involvement in clubs or societies; important people in their lives, people they can rely on; household and family problems and dealing with them; plans for the future; feeling in control, and sources of emotional or practical support.

Topics Directed at the Working Environment Included

Departmental culture, their job, how it compared with their last post and length of service. Attitudes towards and feelings about the job, enjoyable aspects of the work, and whether or not they gain a sense of satisfaction from it.

Difficulties they face with the job or with people at work, and how they cope with them.

Attitudes towards colleagues and working with others; relationships with peers and supervisors; co-operation and trust, and sociability at work.

Daily routine and a typical working day.

Feedback from management.

Feeling in control.

The organisation structure and the individual's place in the hierarchy, whether it is an equitable system.

Their thoughts on the ideal ingredients for a good job.

More General Topics Included

Changes they would like to see which would improve the quality of their lives at work or elsewhere, whether they see a role for themselves in achieving change.

Recent or current health problems affecting their lives in any way.

Experiences or situations in particular which they associate with stress; identifying times when life was particularly good.

Views on whether things which happen in our lives, or the circumstances we find ourselves in, affect our mental health and well-being.

Interviews were carried out in a site of the interviewee's choosing, in the workplace, the interviewee's home, or at the university study site, UCL. A goal of qualitative research is the production of a rich narrative, and a respondent given a choice concerning the location of the interview is more likely to feel in control and at ease, and be more voluble. Respondents were also asked to complete a General Health Questionnaire, later used in analysis to clarify or expand on information on the individual's perceived current mental health status where necessary.

Grounded theory was used in analysis (Strauss & Corbin, 1994). The approach, used successfully in earlier studies, places emphasis on induction, analysis is grounded in the people studied, and analytical categories are expected to emerge. Individual case studies were analysed initially, then theme analysis carried out for each of the three grade groups. Emergent themes—satisfaction and dissatisfaction at work and life outside work, coping strategies and resources, along with meanings and orientations—were adopted as a means of categorising the presentation of analysis. Although names of employment grades have changed in some civil service departments, we use traditional grade titles for consistency when possible, that is, lower grades: Administrative Assistant (AA), Administrative Officer (AO) and clerical (CO); middle grades: Executive Officer (EO), Higher Executive Officer (HEO) and Senior Executive Officer (SEO); and unified (higher) grades 1–7, 7 being the lowest category of higher grade. Names and other identifying features have been anonymised.

References

Allan, G. (1996). *Kinship and Friendship in Modern Britain.* Oxford University Press.

Antonovsky, A. (1987). *Unraveling the Mystery of Health: How People Manage Stress and Stay Well.* Jossey-Bass.

Bhui, K., Stansfeld, S. A., McKenzie, K., Karlsen, S., Nazroo, J., & Weich, S. (2005). Racial/ethnic Discrimination and Common Mental Disorders among Workers: Findings from the EMPIRIC Study of Ethnic Minority Groups in the United Kingdom. *American Journal of Public Health, 3,* 496–501.

Biggs, J. (2015). *All Day Long: A Portrait of Britain at Work.* Serpent's Tale.

Blauner, R. (1964). *Alienation and Freedom.* University of Chicago Press.

Blaxter, M. (1990). *Health and Lifestyles.* Tavistock/Routledge.

Bolton, S. C., & Laaser, K. (2013). Work, Employment and Society Through the Lens of Moral Economy. *Work, Employment and Society, 27*(3), 508–525.

Boxall, P., & Macky, K. (2014). High Involvement Work Processes, Work Intensification and Employee Well-being. *Work, Employment and Society, 28*(6), 963–984.

Breen, K. (2007). Work and Emancipatory Practice: Toward a Recovery of Human Beings' Productive Capacities'. *Res Publica, 1*(3), 381–414.

Brown, G. W., & Harris, T. (1978). *Social Origins of Depression.* Tavistock.

Budd, J. W. (2011). *The Thought of Work.* Cornell Press.

Bulmer, M. (1984). Concepts in the Analysis of Qualitative Data. In M. Bulmer (Ed.), *Sociological Research Methods: An Introduction* (pp. 241–262). Macmillan.

Carter, B., Danford, A., Howcroft, D., Richardson, H., Smith, A., & Taylor, P. (2013). Stressed Out of my Box': Employee Experience of Lean Working and Occupational Ill-health in Clerical Work in the UK Public Sector. *Work, Employment and Society, 27(5) 7,* 47–767.

Castells, M. (1996). *The Rise of Network Society.* Blackwell.

Cattell, V. (2001). Poor People, Poor Places, and Poor Health: The Mediating Role of Social Networks and Social Capital. *Social Science and Medicine, 52*(10), 1501–1516.

Cattell, V. (2003). Social Networks as Mediators Between the Harsh Circumstances of People's Lives and their Lived Experience of Health and Well-being. In C. Phillipson, G. Allan, & D. Morgan (Eds.), *Social Networks and Social Exclusion: Sociological and Policy Perspectives* (pp. 142–161). Ashgate.

Cattell, V. (2004). Having a Laugh and Mucking in Together: Using Social Capital to Explore Dynamics Between Structure and Agency in the Context of Declining and Regenerated Neighbourhoods. *Sociology, 38*(5), 945–963.

Cattell, V. (2012). *Poverty, Community and Health: Co-operation and the Good Society.* Palgrave Macmillan.

Cattell, V., & Evans, M. (1999). *Neighbourhood Images in East London: Social Capital and Social Networks on Two East London Estates.* Joseph Rowntree Foundation.

Cattell, V., & Herring, R. (2002a). Social Capital, Generations and Health in East London. In C. Swann & A. Morgan (Eds.), *Social Capital for Health: Insights from Qualitative Research* (pp. 61–85). Health Development Agency/NICE.

Cattell, V., & Herring, R. (2002b). Social Capital and Well-being: Generations in an East London Neighbourhood. *Journal of Mental Health Promotion, 1*(3), 8–19.

Cieslik, M. (2015). Sociology and the Problem of Happiness. *Sociology, 49*(3), 422–437.

Cohen, S., & Syme, S. L. (Eds.). (1985). *Social Support and Health.* Academic Press.

Crow, G. (2004). Social Networks and Social Exclusion: An Overview of the Debate. In C. Phillipson, G. Allan, & D. Morgan (Eds.), *Social Networks and Social Exclusion: Sociological and Policy Issues* (pp. 7–19). Ashgate.

Cruddas, J. (2021). *The Dignity of Labour.* Polity Press.

Dobson, M., & Schnall, P. L. (2009). From Stress to Distress: The Impact of Work on Mental Health. In P. L. Schnall, M. Dobson, & E. Rosskam (Eds.), *Unhealthy Work: Causes, Consequences, Cures, Baywood* (pp. 113–132). Publishing Company Inc.

Dupois, A., & Thorns, D. C. (1998). Home, Home Ownership and the Search for Ontological Security. *Sociological Review, 46*(1), 24–47.

Elliott, J., Gale, C. R., Parsons, S., & Kuh, D. (2014). Neighbourhood Cohesion and Mental Well-being Among Older Adults. *Social Science and Medicine, 107*, 44–51.

Ferrie, J., Shipley, M., Stansfeld, S. A., et al. (2003). Future Uncertainty and Socioeconomic Inequalities in Health: The Whitehall II Study. *Social Science and Medicine, 57*, 637–651.

Findlay, P., & Thompson, P. (2017). Contemporary Work; Its Meanings and Demands. *Journal of Industrial Relations, 59*(2), 122–138.

Furedi, F. (2004). *Therapy Culture: Cultivating Vulnerability in an Uncertain Age.* Routledge.

Gaillie, D., Felstead, A., & Green, F. (2012). Job Preferences and the Intrinsic Quality of Work: The Changing Attitudes of British Employees 1992–2006. *Work Employment and Society, 26*(5), 806–821.

Gaillie, D., Felstead, A., Green, F., & Inanc, H. (2017). The Hidden Face of Job Insecurity. *Work, Employment and Society, 31*(1), 36–53.

Gatrell, A. C., et al. (2000). Understanding Health Inequalities: Locating people in Geographical and Social Spaces. In *Understanding Health Inequalities* (pp. 156–169). OUP.

Gesler, W. M. (2003). *Healing Places.* Rowman and Littlefield.

Goldberg, D. P., & Hillier, V. F. (1979). A Scaled Version of the General Health Questionnaire. *Psychological Medicine, 9*(1), 139–145.

Goldthorpe, J. H., Lockwood, D., Bechhofer, F., & Platt, J. (1968). *The Affluent Worker: Industrial Attitudes and Behaviour.* Cambridge University Press.

Gomberg, P. (2007). *How to Make Opportunity Equal: Race and Contributory Justice.* Wiley.

Gordon, D. R., & Schnall, P. L. (2009). Beyond the Individual: Connecting Work Environment and Health. In P. L. Schnall, M. Dobson, & E. Rosskam (Eds.), *Unhealthy Work: Causes, Consequences, Cures* (pp. 1–50). Baywood Publishing Company Inc.

Haidt, J. (2006). *The Happiness Hypothesis: Finding Modern Truth in Ancient Wisdom.* Heinemann.

Hammersley, M., & Atkinson, P. (1995). *Ethnography: Principles in Practice.* Routledge.

Health and Safety Executive. (2020). *Work-related Stress, Anxiety or Depression Statistics in Great Britain.* www.hse.gov.uk/statistics

Hildon, Z., Smith, G., Netuveli, G., & Blane, D. (2008). Understanding Adversity and Resilience at Older Ages. *Sociology of Health and Illness, 30*(5), 726–740.

Hoggett, P. (2001). *Agency, Rationality and Social Policy.* Cambridge University Press.

Huppert, F. A. (2009). Psychological Well-being: Evidence Regarding Its Causes and Consequences. *Applied Psychology, Health and Well-being, 1*(2), 137–164.

Jahoda, M. (1982). *Employment and Unemployment: A Social Psychological Analysis.* Cambridge University Press.

Jauregui, M., & Schnall, P. L. (2009). Work, Psychosocial Stressors, and the Bottom Line. In P. L. Schnall, M. Dobson, & E. Rosskam (Eds.), *Unhealthy Work: Causes, Consequences, Cures* (pp. 153–172). Baywood Publishing Company Inc.

Karasek, R. A., & Theorell, T. (1990). *Healthy Work: Stress, Productivity and the Reconstruction of Working Life.* Basic Books.

Kawachi, I., & Berkman, L. F. (2001). Social Ties and Mental Health. *Journal of Urban Health, 78*, 458–467.

Keyes, C. (2002). *Flourishing: Positive Psychology and the Life Well-Lived.* American Psychological Association.

Kirke, D. M. (2006). *Teenagers and Substance Use: Social Networks and Peer Influence.* Palgrave Macmillan.

Kunitz, S. J. (2001). Accounts of Social Capital: The Mixed Health Effects of Personal Communities and Voluntary Groups. In D. Leon & G. Walt (Eds.), *Poverty, Inequality and Health* (pp. 159–174). Oxford University Press.

Layard, R. (2011). *Happiness.* Penguin Books.

Lechner, F. J. (1991). Simmel on Social Space. *Theory Culture and Society, 8*(3), 195–201.

Lucassen, J. (2021). *The Story of Work: A New History of Humankind*. Yale University Press.
Mandemakers, J. J., & Monden, C. W. S. (2013). Does the Effect of Job Loss on Psychological Distress Differ by Educational Level? *Work, Employment and Society, 27*(1), 73–93.
Marmot, M. G., Bosma, H., Hemingway, H., Brunner, E. J., & Stansfeld, S. A. (1997). Contribution of Job Control and Other Risk Factors to Social Variations in Coronary Heart Disease Incidence. *Lancet, 350*, 235–239.
Marmot, M. G., Davey, S. G., Stansfeld, S. A., et al. (1991). Health Inequalities Among British Civil Servants: The Whitehall II Study. *Lancet, 337*, 1387–1393.
Marmot, S. M. (2020). *Health Equity in England: The Marmot Review 10 Years on*. UCL Institute of Health Equity.
Maslow, A. H. (1954). *Motivation and Personality*. Longmans.
Marx (1844/1988). The Economic and Philosophical Manuscripts, Translated by M. Milligan, Prometheus Books.
Mason, P. (2016). *Post Capitalism: A Guide to Our Future*. Penguin.
Mayo, E. (1949). *The Social Problems of an Industrial Civilisation*. Routledge and K. Paul.
McNamara, T. K., Pitt-Catsouphes, M., Matz-Costa, C., Brown, M., & Valcour, M. (2013). Across the Continuum of Satisfaction with Work-family Balance: Work Hours, Flexibility–fit, and Work-Family Culture. *Social Science Research, 42*, 283–298.
Mein, G., Martikainen, P. S., Stansfeld, S. A., Brunner, E. J., Fuhrer, R., & Marmot, M. G. (2000). Predictors of Early Retirement in British Civil Servants. *Age and Aging, 29*, 529–536.
Miech, R. A., & Shanahan, J. (2000). Socioeconomic Status and Depression Over the Life Course. *Journal of Health and Social Behaviour, 41*(2), 162–176.
Mildred, Blaxter. (1990). *Health and Lifestyles*. Routledge.
Montez, J. K., & Friedman, E. M. (2015). Educational Achievement and Adult Health: Under What Conditions Is the Association Causal? *Social Science and Medicine, 127*, 1–7.
Mulligan, M. (2015). On Ambivalence and Hope in the Restless Search for Community in the Global Age. *Sociology, 49*(2), 340–355.
Muntaner, C., Eaton, W.W., Miech, R., & O'Campo, P. (2004). Socioeconomic position and major mental disorders. *Epidemiologic Reviews, 26*, 53–62.
Neal, S., & Murji, K. (2015). Sociologies of Everyday Life: Editors' Introduction to the Special Issue. *Sociology, 49*(5), 811–819.
Office for National Statistics. (2016). *Measuring National Well-being: At what Age Is Personal Well-being the Highest?* www.ons.gov.uk
Pahl, R. (1995). *After Success: Fin de Siecle Anxiety and Identity*. Polity Press.
Pearlin, L. I. (1989). The Sociological Study of Stress. *Journal of Health and Social Behaviour, 30*, 241–256.

Pickering, J. (2001). 'Eco-psychology and Well-being': Paper Presented to the *ESRC Seminar Series on Well-being: Social and Individual Determinants*, London, 11 September, Queen Mary, University of London.

Popay, J., Williams, G., Thomas, C., & Gatrell, A. (1998). Theorizing Inequalities in Health; The Place of Lay Knowledge. In M. Bartley, D. Blane, & G. Davey-Smith (Eds.), *The Sociology of Health Inequalities* (pp. 89–94). Blackwell.

Rose, M. (2003). Good Deal Or Bad Deal: Job Satisfaction in Occupations. *Work Employment and Society, 17*(3), 503–530.

Ryan, R. M., & Deci, E. L. (2001). On Happiness and Human Potential: A Review of Research on Hedonic and Eudaemonic Well-being. *Annual Review of Psychology, 52*, 141–166.

Sandel, M. (2018b). *The Tyranny of Merit: What Became of the Common Good.* Penguin Books.

Savage, M., et al. (2015). *Social Class in the 21st Century.* Pelican.

Sayer, A. (2009). Contributive Justice and Meaningful Work. *Res Publica, 15*(1), 1–16.

Sayer, A. (2011). *Why Things Matter to People: Social Science, Values and Ethical Life.* Cambridge University Press.

Schnall, P. L., Dobson, M., & Rosskam, E. (Eds.). (2009). *Unhealthy Work: Causes, Consequences, Cures.* Baywood Publishing Company Inc.

Sennett, R. (1998). *The Corrosion of Character.* Norton.

Siegrist, J. (1996). Adverse Health Effects of High-effort/Low-reward Conditions. *Journal of Occupational Health Psychology, 1*(1), 27–41.

Skidelsky, L. R., & Glassman, L. M. (2013, October 24). Work as a Value. *LSE Event*, London.

Srnicek, N., & Williams, A. (2015). *Inventing the Future: Post Capitalism and a World Without Work.* Verso Books.

Stansfeld, S. A., & Candy, B. (2006). Psychosocial Work Environment and Mental Health – A Meta-analytical Review. *Scandinavian Journal of Work Environment and Health, 32*(6), 443–462.

Stansfeld, S. A., Fuhrer, R., Shipley, M. J., & Marmot, M. G. (1999). Work Characteristics Predict Psychiatric Disorder: Prospective Results from the Whitehall II Study. *Occupational and Environmental Medicine, 56*(5), 302–307.

Stansfeld, S. A., Head, J., Cattell, V., Wardle, J., & Fuhrer, R. (2004). Partner's Employment Status and Depressive Symptoms in Women. *Trends in Evidence based Neuropsychiatry, 6*(1), 31–36.

Stansfeld, S. A., Head, J., Fuhrer, R., Wardle, J., & Cattell, V. (2003). Social Inequalities in Depressive Symptoms and Physical Functioning in the Whitehall II Study: Exploring a Common Cause Explanation. *Journal of Epidemiology and Community Health, 57*(5), 361–367.

Stansfeld, S. A., Head, J., & Marmot, M. G. (1998). Explaining Social Class Differences in Depression and Well-being. *Social Psychiatry and Psychiatric Epidemiology, 33*, 1–9.

Stansfeld, S. A., Shipley, M., Head, J., Fuhrer, R., & Kivimaki, M. (2013). Work Characteristics and Personal Social Support as Determinants of Subjective Well-being. *PLoS One, 8*(11), e81115.

Strangleman, T. (2012). Work Identity in Crisis? Rethinking the Problem of Attachment and Loss at Work. *Sociology, 46*(3), 411–425.

Strauss, A., & Corbin, J. (1994). Grounded Theory Methodology: An Overview. In N. Denzin & Y. S. Lincoln (Eds.), *Handbook of Qualitative Research* (pp. 273–285). Sage.

Taylor, M. (2021). *Do We Have to Work? A Primer for the 21st Century.* Thames and Hudson.

Thomas, W. I., & Thomas, D. (1929). *The Child in America.* Alfred Knopf.

Turner, R. J., Wheaton, B., & Lloyd, D. A. (1995). The Epidemiology of Social Stress. *American Sociological Review, 60*(1), 104–125.

Valente, T. W. (2010). *Social Networks and Health: Models, Methods and Applications.* Oxford University Press.

Vogt, K. C. (2016). The Post-Industrial Society: From Utopia to Ideology. *Work, Employment and Society, 30*(2), 366–376.

Warhurst, C., Carre, F., & Tilly, C. (Eds.). (2012). *Are Bad Jobs Inevitable? Trends, Determinants and Responses to Job Quality in the Twenty First Century.* Palgrave Macmillan.

Weeks, K. (2011). *The Problem with Work.* Duke University Press.

Wellman, B., & Wortley, S. (1990). Different Strokes from Different Folks: Community Ties and Social Support. *American Journal of Sociology, 96*(3), 558–588.

Whelan, C. (1993). The Role of Social Support in Mediating the Psychological Consequences of Economic Stress. *Sociology of Health and Illness, 15*(1), 86–101.

WHO. (2001). *The World Health Report – Mental Health: New Understandings, New Hope.* WHO.

WHO. (2018). *The World Health Report.* WHO.

World Health Organisation (WHO). (1948). *Constitution.* WHO.

Ziersch, A. M., Baum, F. E., MacDougall, C., & Putland, C. (2004). Neighbourhood Life and Social Capital: The Implications for Health. *Social Science and Medicine, 60*(1), 71–86.

Zou, M. (2015). Gender, Work Orientation and Job Satisfaction. *Work, Employment and Society, 29*(1), 3–22.

CHAPTER 2

Lower Grades and Social Relations

Abstract Based on rich narratives, our findings demonstrate grade variation as well as commonality in the breadth and kinds of stressors experienced and resources available to people in their working lives and outside paid employment and consider some of the meanings invested in them. Particular stressors deriving from the workplace can be more common in lower grades, performing new tasks without adequate training was experienced as stressful, for example, as were difficult relationships, communication problems, uncertainty about the future, dysfunctional work units, and feeling alienated from the working environment. Some potential difficulties were not necessarily viewed as a problem if they gained enjoyment from other aspects of the job. The most prominent feature of this grade group concerned the primacy of experiencing good social relations and friendly and supportive social ties at work and outside work. Changes in the social organisation of the workplace could result in negative effects on satisfaction and on mental health and well-being. Examples of particularly acute perceptions of powerlessness amongst lower grades were linked to, for example, an inability to settle a problem because help was not available, and feeling alienated from the work tasks and from colleagues.

Keywords Social relations • Satisfaction • Work • Powerlessness • Depression • Dysfunctional • Well-being: Alienation • Bullying • Coping

V. Cattell, S. Stansfeld, *Work in the Balance*,
https://doi.org/10.1007/978-3-031-96582-1_2

This qualitative research has illustrated some of the ways in which both stressors and resources are not only socially distributed and experienced but also interpreted and understood by men and women in different civil service grades. Adopting a holistic approach to the research has placed us in a better position to understand why some people and not others in given circumstances feel out of control or become anxious and depressed.

Across employment grades civil servants talked about aspects of work and life outside which they found satisfying and fulfilling, and those which they found problematic and stressful, and identified factors which ameliorated or exacerbated stressful experience. This and the next two chapters discuss these alongside different levels of meaning invested in them.

Whilst the lower grade group included house owners, interviews also indicated that renting homes (privately and socially) and living in flats, as expected, were more common for lower grades taking part in the study than for people in middle and higher grades. Though not a widespread experience for these public servants, material resources inadequate for needs—such as poor housing, a low income, experiencing debt, or living in a neighbourhood with declining facilities—were confirmed as sources of stress for certain individuals in lower grades. Restricted by low income and physical incapacity, living in an area of decline characterised by loss of local work and facilities, and by out migration, a lower grade man for example had little hope for the future and appeared anxious, depressed, and defeated. A woman whose many workplace problems contributed to her depression, lived on a highly deprived estate, had no pleasant neighbourhood surroundings to act as a buffer to her difficulties, and a lack of neighbourhood trust reduced neighbourly interaction and reciprocity. For many others, especially but not exclusively women, however, the immediate locality, involving ties of family, neighbours, and friends, was viewed positively and plays an important role in their lives.

Sources of Job Satisfaction

Aspects of the work task itself, its skills content for example, was rarely elaborated on in relation to satisfaction and enjoyment amongst those interviewed in this grade group. There were a variety of alternative sources of satisfaction identified, nonetheless. Some respondents focus simply on completing their work at the end of the day and, occasionally, on pride derived from receiving acknowledgement that a job is well done. Others looked to extraneous features such as appreciation of the part of London they worked in, or less tangible workplace qualities which, though found much less frequently for civil servants on lower grades, included a sense of proprietorship and identity with the job. An unusual example for this grade group is related to appreciation and perceptions of ownership of the assets of the workplace and a sense of commitment to the organisation. Mr Young, a supervisor of museum attendants described what he loved about his job: 'When we locked up at night it was ours, we protected it, no matter what'.

Despite very few exceptions, such as Mr Teller (CO), for example, who preferred working out of the way in an office where he would not have to deal with people, and another CO, Mr Fellowes, who expressed little sympathy towards the claimants he dealt with, where jobs could involve contact with members of the public, lower grades generally derive pleasure from being able to assist them, and value the expressions of appreciation they receive in return. Most frequently however, narratives on satisfaction centred on good social relations with colleagues, whether peers or bosses. There are many on administrative and clerical grades who appreciate being able to interact with others as part of their daily routine or who enjoy socialising with colleagues—as a female AO, Mrs George, expressed it: 'I get round to see almost everybody, the satisfaction I get from work is mainly from talking to people'—and who recognise benefits in social interaction at work in building the trusting relationships necessary for workplace co-operation or support. Work can be a source of pleasure for these civil servants, people like Mrs Yardley for example, who spoke in glowing terms of the friendliness and good humour of her work group: 'I like meeting people; I like to have some fun at work … we have a laugh'. Additionally, opportunities to mix beyond as well as within the work section or unit can be helpful for promoting well-being through facilitating support and advice. Seeing former colleagues at the tea point for example provides an opportunity to approach them for information.

An illustration of the value attached to good relations with effective supervisors is provided by an AO who had begun her career at a lower level and who spoke very positively about her job throughout her interview. Mrs George expressed gratitude for the way line managers had assisted her career. For others, such as secretaries to senior officials especially, a good relationship with their boss, often someone they admired, was key to their job satisfaction.

Dissatisfaction at Work

People in lower grades reported experiencing dissatisfaction at work associated with a wide variety of factors including routine; career issues and promotion; poor relations with line managers (mentioned frequently); communications problems; perceptions of workplace injustice; dysfunctional work units and poor social relations along with difficulties coping with change such as tackling new technologies or disruption of the work group. A combination of stressors occurring together was experienced as particularly damaging.

There were surprisingly relatively fewer complaints than expected on the routine nature of the work undertaken, or on its lack of variety, but examples included a man who described his work as 'tedious, dull, and mind numbing. It left me exhausted' (Mr Fellowes, CO). He reported that he had always felt entirely unsuited to his job however, because 'You had to conform to the system and could not act independently'. While a few of our respondents did mention having some variety in their jobs in positive terms, contrary to expectations, we found that it was not always the case that variation in the routine tasks carried out was appreciated. One man for example, acknowledging that his job and Ministry held very little interest for him explained: 'We used to swap jobs at one time. …, but then gradually you get to hate all the jobs rather than just one job' (Mr Teller, C O).

Lack of Promotion, Annual Reports, and Negative Feedback

Many of the lower grades taking part in the study don't generally have issues with the grade system as such, at least when they see it as working well, although several nonetheless complained about being passed over for promotion, something which was generally interpreted as unjust. Mr Boyle (CO), for example, who had enjoyed his job as a civil servant, liking the security and the work itself and appreciating his work friends, became very angry however when he was overlooked for a promotion he had expected. He left the Service because of this, something which he later very much regretted. In another case, Mr Trafford (AO), who gains little in the way of job satisfaction overall, felt 'very bitter' when colleagues with fewer qualifications were promoted above him; he suggested that racial prejudice may have been a contributory factor. The situation is particularly galling for Mr Trafford as he sees his contemporaries—who like him, came to this country from overseas several decades ago—now doing well.

While receiving positive feedback from line managers was welcome, a common grievance, and one not restricted to lower grades, concerned overly negative feedback via annual reports and the distress this caused them. For example: 'They [his superiors] took you to bits, they never gave you credit for your successes' (Mr Fellowes, CO). Describing the stress he had felt under at these times he added: 'They sent for a welfare officer, but I didn't know why I was seeing him. I was just so cut off'. An added issue here was that his report assessment seemed to confirm what he already felt about his unsuitability for the work: he had little confidence in his abilities and felt that he was not sufficiently academic. A woman who considered the system to be especially unfair, when interviewed, was feeling constantly under strain. She too insisted that: 'They need to get rid of the annual reports. … They screw people up every time' (Mrs McBride). She described herself as hardworking and considered her treatment to be unjust. Her account reflects a perceived effort/reward imbalance: 'I'm working long hours to impossible deadlines, and he gives me a low mark on my annual report. It's insulting' (Mrs McBride). The importance of the role and behaviour of supervisors in this context was also highlighted by others participating in the study. An AO, for example, insisted that: 'The reporting system only works if you are working for decent people'. Whilst her present line manager: 'is very good and gives you a report that you'd probably write for yourself', the previous one: 'put down things that weren't true in the report … and he was racist. I used to be all tensed up because of him'. Referring to the powerlessness she felt at that time she added: 'It's only one man's opinion against yours' (Mrs Hart, AO).

Poor Social Relations and Conflict

Poor social relations and conflict, with line managers especially, were issues which came up relatively frequently as sources of dissatisfaction, underlining their importance to mental health outcomes. When interviewed, Mrs McBride, mentioned above, had just requested transfer to another section. She, along with co-workers, found her boss very difficult. His allegedly erratic behaviour (he may well have had mental health problems himself) and what she considered to be the unreasonable demands he placed on her, was causing Mrs McBride considerable stress. Her GHQ responses confirmed that she was feeling constantly under strain.

In another example, a photocopying assistant, Miss Norden (AA), took early retirement following her experience in what she described as a dysfunctional work unit and a very poor relationship with her supervisor. She was able to draw on a great deal of support from family and friends outside the workplace to help her cope, but noted that other, less fortunate colleagues in the same unit had suffered from stress related illness including depression. The relationship between Miss Snell (AO) with her supervisor was also especially unsatisfactory: he was reportedly heavily critical of the work of his subordinates. Miss Snell was reprimanded, for example, over not dealing with some files at a time when she felt overloaded with work, a situation exacerbated by chronic physical health problems. A co-incidence of stressful events here left her with little strength to deal with the work situation, and consequently resulted in her feeling out of control. When communication problems in the department made the situation almost impossible to rectify: 'it was difficult to get over to management that we found him difficult', this worsened her distress, she felt 'completely out of control', and was left feeling: 'emotionally bruised'.

Additional examples of perceptions of powerlessness, often connected with perceived organisational injustice and the friction it can cause, concerned a supervisor who reportedly presented her subordinates' ideas to management as her own: 'We didn't complain because we felt powerless' explained Miss Norden (AA). Feeling powerless within the structure of a particular work unit impacted on the ability of civil servants like her to solve a work problem, whilst an inability to rectify the problematic situation reinforced perceptions of powerlessness. Ms Drummond (AA) felt in a similarly weak position and powerless to address serious work problems. A previous supervisor, of whom she spoke admiringly, was replaced by someone who allegedly made fun of her, passed her over for promotion, and hid her report. Ms Drummond's attempts to get help appeared to fall on deaf ears: 'The union wouldn't help, neither would management; … the union is on their side'. She added: 'I don't bother myself now, because you will never win'. For some individuals, a personal *need* for being in control was also apparent. When people leave their job, whether moving on to another post in the Service, or going outside altogether, relocating can help them clarify what they find satisfying or dissatisfying about work, and why. A man who recognised his own need for tight control over how the work should be carried out, chose to leave because of conflict with his seniors over the most appropriate way to do the job.

As well as good social relations simply not existing in a particular unit, it was also where they were disrupted by re-organisation that the workplace became a source of stress and poor well-being. Staffing changes, involving dislocation of supports for example, could be expected to have a greater impact on lower grade staff—who tended to value them highly—than on those in higher grades. Ms Drummond's experience of multiple changes involving staff and shifts, meant that what she used to enjoy about her job, that is, the sociability of her work mates, and 'knowing what was going on', no longer existed. Mr Jones, a supervisor of attendants who was moved to a new post, described the disunity and distrust between the men and between management and men on his shift. He found the situation particularly distressing because up until then, he had always worked with 'a great load of blokes'. There was also some evidence of a precipitation of stressors occurring under these circumstances. The same man was suspended following an incident which, in more cohesive circumstances or with a more 'hands on' and supportive management, would, he believed, have been more likely to have been resolved. The suspension was causing him a great deal of anxiety: 'Some of the stress is coming from management. I've been there for three months but the first time I spoke to the head man was when they wanted to suspend me. It's awful that. He hadn't bothered to introduce himself to me before' (Mr Jones).

Stability, Change, and Disintegration of the Workgroup

Stability, change, and coping with change, mentioned already in connection with co-operative social relations, were common themes across different aspects of the research findings. Anticipating the move to a new building for example, can cause people to feel unsettled or anxious, while unsuccessful attempts to cope with new technology without receiving adequate training could leave people like Mrs Noble (AA) for example feeling foolish. She reported that she worried to the extent that she no longer enjoyed her job. Mr Jones, mentioned earlier, was promoted to supervisor, a post necessitating relocation. He was feeling out of control and under stress as a result of this and because he had not received any training for the new job. He explained that: 'normally when people get made up to a supervisor they had started on the bottom and learned everything, [but here] there's a lot of things that I haven't learned, and will never know, and I don't even know my way around the building'. Referring to his suspension, he added: 'It's difficult enough learning a new job at my age. You have all these new things to learn, new alarms, new computer systems and without all of this [his suspension] as well' (Mr Jones).

Whilst being relocated and having to cope with additional changes can lead to feelings of losing control, the part played by the relative stability of the work group was a feature of most narratives on attitudes to change and coping with it. A post room supervisor, Mrs Yardley, described how having to do new tasks for example, was made easier in her unit in a context of a co-operative work culture and practices. When new tasks and an added workload are combined with disruption of routines *and* disruption of the social organisation of the unit (as in Mr Jones's case), consequent health problems appeared almost inevitable. Ms Drummond (AA) described a time when staffing numbers were reduced. She was moved from building to building and was unfamiliar with the working practices of the different locations. She felt overwhelmed and out of control trying to cope with too many tasks, and new tasks, to a particular time scale. The situation worsened when the Department employed agency staff to replace those they had cut and training them became an additional burden for the remaining regulars. There were further disruptions to the stability of the work group when shifts underwent repeated changes. Taken together, she was describing a context in which it had become impossible for people to support each other, a situation which exacerbated the additional stress the assistant was put under when she was bullied by a new supervisor. She became depressed and when interviewed, had not worked since.

A Co-incidence of Stressors

Ms Drummond's recall of her experience of multiple stressors at work, related above, focused on feeling overwhelmed together with strong perceptions of losing control: 'We had to do more work, we had to go to different buildings and every building was different, it was confusing. … We *have* to do the work; we *have* to get everything out by a certain time. We *have* to deal with this, we *have* to deal with that, and we *have* to train them [the temps] and they don't know nothing. … This is why so many people are sick from here. … And then they changed the shifts' (Ms Drummond, AA). Her distress did not stop when she left at the end of a shift: 'It just breaks you up, it's just torn you apart, you get sick over it. … You are only getting paid for 40 hours, but you are taking the worry home with you'. Ms Drummond is convinced that work-related stress made her ill, both physically (with raised blood pressure) and mentally. The episode left her feeling fatalistic. Feeling fatalistic and out of control was reflected in her attitude to illness: 'When illness comes on you there is nothing anyone can do about it anyway ... and the stress builds up on you'. Having sought help from her union but without success, her discomfort was exacerbated by her inability to do anything to improve the situation.

Coinciding stressors (a term used by Pearlin, 1989) and their negative impacts are not of course restricted to those experienced in the workplace. Problems with one area of one's life, such as uncertainty about future working arrangements, can lead to feelings of loss of control, effects which can be exacerbated when combined with difficulties in other areas of life. Mr Boyle's (CO) multiple difficulties, for example, were derived from both work and home, and from uncertainty and change in both. Redundancies are threatened in the organisation he now works for since recently having left the Civil Service, and his strong desire to move house is partly dependant on the co-operation of relatives. His family appears to be a dysfunctional one in many respects and is a source of great anxiety for him. Problems at home make him feel: 'low, very, very low'. In addition, he sincerely regrets having left the Civil Service, which he described as one big happy family, and misses his old job: 'When I think of the old job and the minor squabbles we had, it was *paradise* compared to this [new job]. He reported feeling suicidal at times, equally depressed at home and at work. It was the co-incidence of stressful experiences, of multiple traumas, at this point in time which, he felt, led to the depression he was being treated for when interviewed. When talking about work problems he would then switch to talking about home difficulties and vice versa. A strong sense of loss comes across from the interview, and a desire to return to happier places, happier times. He worries about possible losses in the future also, particularly the loss of his pets, to whom he is close. He added, 'I have contemplated suicide quite a few times. The reason why I don't do it is because I feel if I kill myself, I won't be with my dead pets'.

Protecting Well-Being: Factors Mitigating Negative Experience and Stress

A diverse range of factors, whether from within the workplace or from other domains of respondents' lives, emerged as important influences on the extent to which generally negatively perceived work characteristics and situations were recounted and experienced as stressful. They included support at work or at home; leading a balanced life; gaining satisfaction from other aspects of their work; good communications in the workplace, and the various meanings that work held for individuals.

Support

When there's a sudden increase in work, which may involve starting a job and then having to switch to another, more urgent one, fortunate employees can call on others to give them a hand if they are not too busy themselves. Co-operative help amongst peers is generally predicated on good social relations amongst staff. Mrs George: 'knows everybody' and likes her colleagues; a sense of her solidarity with them is reflected in her repeated use of the word 'we' and not 'I' throughout her interview. Being able to access support regularly, consistently, and reliably was considered essential by some respondents. If Mrs George has any work related or other problems she can talk to a friend in her section whom she has worked with for 14yrs; if people in Mr Teller's (CO), unit need information, they can ask 'A guy in the office who has been there 15 yrs', experiences which call attention to advantages associated with continuity in staffing arrangements.

Support from supervisors and bosses is likely to be especially important for the well-being of people in lower grades, not only because their tasks may necessitate a greater degree of supervision, but also because good social relations at work can be invested with a strong meaning for them. A senior secretary, Mrs Tully, reported that she has always been able to sort out problems by 'working in a well organised department for a boss who takes the concerns of his staff seriously'. Others interviewed also stressed their appreciation of approachable line managers and having good communications in place when they need information or, like Mrs Andrews (AO), wish to 'get their point of view across'. Mrs Morgan (AO), described the reciprocal relationship she has with her supervisors who allow her to take unanticipated leave for family emergencies and do so because they recognised that she puts a lot into the job, is prepared to work overtime, and helps organise social celebrations at work.

Alongside work contacts, civil servants mentioned friends, family and community ties, and their role as important sources of social support for alleviating difficulties encountered at work. Friends included those made in previous jobs, valuable assets for discussing current work problems.

Many others spoke of their family and community networks and the role they played in helping them cope with work related and other difficulties. Our interviewees also recounted ways in which they could access practical and emotional support from workmates for problems encountered outside the workplace. Mr Thomas's (AA) wife was seriously ill in hospital, and he was feeling out of control of the situation: 'Strokes are unpredictable things' he said. His expressions of helplessness were shared by others in this grade group when trying to cope with family illness. In his case, people at work as well as helpful neighbours were assisting Mr Thomas in getting through it. Supervisors, managers, and personnel officers were accommodating, arranging for him to work part time for example. In describing his relationships with his immediate colleagues, he said: '[T]hey're not intrusive but if you are in need, they will help you. Knowing that someone will listen to your problems is good, knowing that yes, you can trust people'.

Support for Multiple Stressors

People with a multitude of problems in their lives may need multiple forms of support. Although accessing it was not a universal experience for people on lower grades by any means, there were exceptions. Almost all the major spheres of Mr Boyle's (CO) life—his family, home, neighbourhood, and work—are, as we have seen, a source of unhappiness, stress, and anxiety, but supportive friends were seeing him through this difficult phase of his life, providing him with advice and consolation and listening when he was feeling very low: 'and if wasn't for my friends and my doctor and my pets I wouldn't want to be alive'. His girlfriend is a calming influence on him, and consequently, he was starting to feel more hopeful. His response to a question on perceptions of control for example focused on his plans for the future, he was beginning to take steps to rectify some of the situations he finds himself in: 'As long as I take it one step at a time, I feel I can be in control'.

Mr Young is under considerable strain resulting from a tortuous home life and is heavily in debt, but he gains regular help from a group of workmates who have set up informal meetings for mutual assistance. This, together with support from his wider family, 'they back me no matter what', from outside agencies, and from the counselling he receives, made him able to say that he is coping well. Although his GHQ responses indicate a relatively low mood and some anxiety, he nevertheless displayed a strong determination 'not to go under'. Before he began to access support, he felt out of control: 'Debt was leading me. Now I am taking control and can see an end to it'. He links feeling in control with taking action to sort out personal problems.

The Importance of Social Networks as Resources

Although social ties can sometimes be problematic, social ties—family, colleagues, and friends—were a key source of practical and emotional support, and especially important in the lives of lower grades. While there were examples of individuals (notably men) across grades who said they were content with relatively small networks, there were also examples of people where restricted networks were recognised as detracting from their quality of life. Those individuals in lower grades who saw themselves as relatively isolated or lonely included people low on additional resources or people who had recently experienced negative life events. They included, firstly, a single man, Mr Connolly (AO), who had cared for his elderly mother for many years in an unsuitable flat, whose social activities had been restricted by his caring role, and who was now alone. Secondly, a woman living alone whose three oldest, closest, and most supportive friends—met when she first moved to this country—had all recently died, and who lived in an area with a very high resident turnover where she knew no one and 'Everybody keeps themselves to themselves' (Mrs Hart, AO). She described the deep sense of loss she felt following the death of one particular friend, it was a long-term friendship based on shared experience, an invaluable coping resource for past difficulties. Thirdly, a man limited by physical illness, Mr Downs, who lives in a run-down housing estate where most of his local acquaintances have moved on or died. In his case especially he has few options to widen his networks to help him cope with illness. He can't ask neighbours for help because 'we don't know them now'. A sense of loss comes across, much of it centred on enjoyable social interaction. He used to go to the pub for a drink, but the medication he is on now prevents that, while in any case there are also few traditional working men's pubs left in the area. The quality of existing ties assumes especial importance in such circumstances. He and his wife try to support each other but worry about each other too. Both suffer from depression.

All three of these individuals live in rented accommodation in places they have no strong attachment to and don't have the financial resources to relocate elsewhere. They reported feeling, or having recently felt, low, or under stress. We might expect all three to be at risk of depression, but their cases illustrate also the importance of work and workplacc tics as a positive resource and a help or buffer for difficulties elsewhere. The man whose mother died, for example, Mr Connolly (AO), had a history of long-term health difficulties including depression but colleagues and supervisors were sympathetic and did not overburden him when he was feeling under stress. Work came as a relief while co-operative work practices gave him a sense of satisfaction derived from a feeling that he could help. Mr Downs, the last case, was no longer working however, and as can be common with working-class men who no longer remain in the context in which their friendships were made (see Allan, 1996) has not retained contact with his work mates. Whilst the local community can, for some people, be a source of new friendships, in his case physical changes, gentrification, and out migration meant that it did not have the capacity to compensate for their loss. Work elsewhere which has looked at loneliness (Independent Age, 2014) indicated that men with poor health, low incomes, few qualifications, and living in rented housing are hit hardest by loneliness.

Where home problems are supported and capable of resolution, we could expect perhaps a cushioning effect whereby the individual is better able to cope with negative work issues. Confirming earlier work on community life and the associated benefits for well-being (Cattell, 2001, 2003), there were examples in the present study of where living in a stable, co-operative neighbourhood had both direct benefits and aided coping with difficulties at home, such as caring responsibilities. The dislocation of local ties, though affecting people across grades, for lower grade individuals can also be more difficult to rectify and render health effects potentially more serious. The case of Mr Downs for example, who saw the value of having local ties but who lived in an area of rapid change where it was almost impossible to maintain them and who does not have the financial or other resources to improve his situation, can be contrasted with that of a higher grade man, mentioned in Chap. 4, who, after moving from an area where he had many contacts, has the resources which enable him to address the loss of his former ties. Relocating to a pleasant (and expensive) part of London, he found there were plentiful opportunities for local social involvement.

A Balanced Life

A life built around work and family can contribute to achieving a work/ life balance, but close-knit family networks for example, can sometimes have limitations. When Ms North's mother, to whom she is very close, had a stroke, Ms North phoned one of her siblings, but he collapsed himself with the shock and was unable to help. Though access to wider networks is less common in lower grades, some civil servants like Mr Young and Mr Thomas discussed earlier, are amongst those in the fortunate position of being able to access support from different domains of their lives. Additional cases included Miss Carter (AA) a recently bereaved woman who gained emotional support from her close church friends and from the woman she sits next to at work. The same colleague could be accessed for help with work issues, as could her racial equality mentor. References made by civil servants to different arenas of everyday life not only touch on support available, however. Where experience of and attitudes towards one domain are positive, coping with difficulties in another is assisted through cushioning stress, or by simply acting as a distraction. Mrs Drew, a secretary, described how work was able to buffer personal problems when she felt low: 'You've got people you are relating to all the time'. Similarly, Mrs Tully, a senior secretary, understood the role of work as a distraction for her at difficult times, such as when her mother was ill: 'The job kept me sane, you had to get on with life'. This function attributed to work could be especially invaluable for those few people in the study who did not seek social support readily. Miss Snell (AA), for example would not ask anyone for support when feeling 'quite depressed' when her father died, or indeed for work issues which she had difficulty with. She explained that she had been lonely as a child, and her mother's poor health had made childhood an anxious time for her. Although she did not feel able to confide in anybody, just being at work helped her to 'push it [her father's death] to the back of my mind'. In a similar case, Mrs Sadler did not try to seek emotional support at work when feeling low following her mother's death, explaining that security issues relating to her husband's job meant that she learnt to 'keep herself to herself', but recognised that work nevertheless acted as a diversion from her problems.

From an opposite perspective, an active life outside work, by acting as a distraction (though we found fewer cases here than in middle grades), helped protect an atypical lower grade civil servant from experiencing poor mental well-being resulting from what could be quite serious problems at work. Miss Norden (AA) explained that she coped with a worrying work situation not only by accessing support from her many contacts, but also by keeping active outside work during the evenings and at weekends, through involvement in the social activities of her church for example. She added: '[Y]ou have to if you live alone, I will not let work affect my mental health'.

Factors Moderating Negative Aspects of Specific Work Characteristics

Lower grade civil servants talked about workplace factors acting to mitigate specific negative work characteristics such as routine, dull work, overload, or lack of promotion. Routine work was not always necessarily perceived as a problem but tolerated by respondents in particular contexts, such as when having interesting material to file, where there are informal social distractions, or where they were able to gain satisfaction from other aspects of work. For Mrs Noble (AA), for example, being able to cope with the job without too much hassle, a decent supervisor and companionable colleagues along with convenient hours, appeared to more than compensate for the tedious nature of her work. For another, Mrs George (AO), enjoyable social distractions involving 'talking to people, having a laugh with them' made her day go faster. Problems like routine work or a lack of promotion appear as relatively unproblematic especially in cases where benefits derived from other aspects of the job hold greater significance for some individuals. Mr Thomas (Attendant) was not interested in gaining promotion, as it would incur working in an office, away from working with people, which he loves. Mrs Andrews (AO) reported that for her, social relationships are key: 'Work can be boring and repetitive at times, but helping the public to find work is satisfying, and I've made a lot of friends in the civil service—that's a big bonus for me'. While positive and satisfying aspects of work like these could offset negative features, in an unusual case, it was his thorough dislike of his workplace as a whole, his alienation from it, which affected a CO's attitude towards promotion. He had a very low opinion of the people he would be supervising for example and so turned down promotion opportunities.

Meanings of Work

Various emotional meanings invested in work, and their derivation, emerged as particularly strong influences on the extent to which characteristics of work generally perceived negatively, such as overwork, lack of promotion, or dull and routine work, are considered a problem and reported as stressful. A heavy workload for example was not a problem for Mrs York (AA), if her work was appreciated. In such circumstances, she was able to feel in control even when overburdened. As Sayer has argued, we can be dependent on the valuation of others for our self-esteem and respect (Sayer, 2011). When moving into a larger branch where people did not know her reputation for efficiency and careful work however, Mrs York suffered a resulting loss of confidence. Her need for feeling appreciated, grew, she believed, from a lonely and unhappy childhood—a highly critical mother, a violent father, and no siblings.

A lack of confidence could affect attitudes to promotion. Many of the lower grades in the study (women especially) remain quite content with the way their careers have gone. For example: 'I've been very happy in the grade, I don't feel as though I am a square peg in a round hole' said Ms North (AA). She explained that she would not like to move to a clerical grade partly because, like others already mentioned, she would lose the contact with people which she enjoyed, but also because she considered herself to be 'not gradey, not very brainy'. While a lack of promotion did not appear to be an issue in cases where secretaries viewed their position as outside the competitive grade system, one, Mrs Dalton had cause for complaint. She greatly admired her boss, a woman who had moved up the career ladder since Mrs Dalton had started working for her, but while Mrs Dalton's own duties had considerably expanded in tandem, her pay grade had not changed. She felt that her boss had let her down, a situation which she found especially hurtful, not simply because she felt she had been treated unjustly, but also because she admired her so much.

Mr Case (AA) was amongst those especially disappointed by their own lack of promotion; Mr Case came to England as a young man hoping and expecting to better himself. In contrast, despite remaining on the same relatively low grade throughout his quite long Civil Service career, something which for others can be a source of disquiet, Mr Blay (AO) was contented. Work met his overarching need for status. He perceived his job positively, as a 'high quality job' and one which carries responsibility. Younger colleagues, he reports, respect him, recognise his accumulated knowledge and ask his advice. The content of the job itself, which required him to contact managers of firms, played an additional part in reinforcing his position as one of high status: '[Y]ou go right to the top'.

Life Orientation

When considering different layers of meaning, we looked at the significance that work holds in relation to an individual's overall life orientation (see Goldthorpe et al., 1968), which here refers to the strength of the meanings which different aspects of life hold. The following cases illustrate the part played by differing individual perspectives and include a predominant focus on life outside work, on actively improving things, on status, and, especially, on social relations.

Orientation: Life Outside Work

For some lower grade civil servants, the main focus of their lives lies outside work altogether, their affective needs are met elsewhere though family, neighbourhood, social, or other activity. Mrs York's (AA) case for example was not untypical of some female respondents in this grade group. It was family life, not work, which was central in meeting her needs: 'My relationship with my husband and family are more important than anything. I didn't have a happy childhood, that's why I focus on family now'. For her, and for the following example, potential problems like a lack of promotion were simply not an issue, she happily remained a part time assistant in a job which was convenient for her family responsibilities. Another was Mrs Noble (AA), for whom social activities involving her husband and long-term friends were a pivotal aspect of her life. Working part time had made it easier for her to maintain these friendships.

The life orientation of Mr Teller, (CO), also lay firmly outside the workplace. He gained little satisfaction from work, but a great deal from his membership of an organisation related to his hobby. He is not ambitious, does not expect work to be fulfilling, and acknowledged that the work of his Ministry held little interest for him. Consequently, problems at work seemed unlikely to cause him distress, nor did those in his home, family, or neighbourhood: he does not expect to derive satisfaction from any of these areas but only from the hobby club. Things going wrong at the club, or people there behaving other than he would wish did however cause him to become very angry or upset. His sense of hopelessness here, in relation to most aspects of his job and his home may also have been affected by his father's recent death, but he would be unlikely to acknowledge it.

As we have seen, when interviewed, pets were the primary focus of Mr Boyle's (CO) life. He is very unhappy both at work and at home, where he shares a house with disagreeable relatives. He has no affection for his present neighbourhood either, considering it a danger to his pets. These he describes as his lifeline; they cropped up in conversation relating to every aspect of his life. While pets bring him comfort, their welfare is also a source of worry and sadness. Knowing that they are safe, the happiest part of his day is when he goes to sleep with his animals all around him. He acknowledged that a tragic and traumatic boyhood memory involving the death of a pet helped explain his investment in relationships with animals, and his anxiety about them. He realises that he has ambivalent emotions about pets and finds it very hard to cope (including at work) when they become ill and die. His strong feelings could have a damaging effect on relationships at work. On one occasion, when his boss asked him to come into work, Mr Boyle told him where to go in no uncertain terms and added: '[M]y baby is dead and I want to bury her, and I want to be with her, that's how I feel'.

Orientation: Action

An orientation involving a commitment to taking action to improve working life or local circumstances was much less common amongst lower grades taking part in the study than it was, for example, for middle grades, but a striking exception can be noted. Portrayals of both her experience of work and her local neighbourhood reflect Miss Carter's (AA) strong commitment to take action to improve the circumstances of her life and signify the satisfaction and sense of empowerment she gained from her successes. She regularly addresses casual racism at work, and she challenged a new, and noisy, open plan office layout which colleagues found stressful: 'People at the top drew up the plans. They had nice offices near the windows, and we were left without enough partitions for privacy. So … I made it clear we wanted something done'. Miss Carter, together with her colleagues rejected several proposed alterations until they achieved something more acceptable to them. Outside of work, she is heavily involved in groups campaigning (and succeeding) to improve local conditions and derives a sense community from her activities as well as empowerment.

Orientation: Status

His work, as we saw earlier, but also his outside activities meet Mr Blay's (AO) paramount need and appetite for status. Layard (2005) argues that making comparisons with others who are more successful than ourselves can make us discontented. Mr Blay however evaluates and rationalises various aspects of his life—his career, family, neighbourhood, outside activities, and income—in relation to similar others, both here and in his country of birth. He is able to interpret his position in relation to them in a positive light. He believes that he has achieved a greater status than contemporaries who emigrated to the UK when he did but are still employed in factories, and is financially better off than friends who remained abroad, where they achieved high status jobs, but whose pay is lower than his. These people, he reports, see him as of a higher standing than themselves. He gains additional kudos from his social networks in the UK derived from 'mixing with senior, powerful people', and rooted in his participation in an Anglo-X society.

Whilst Mr Blay's general outlook can be expected to be beneficial to his job satisfaction and sense of well-being, a status orientation can be harmful in some circumstances. Some senior secretaries taking part in the study appreciate and derive their own sense of status from the contact they have with higher grade colleagues, and identity with them. Ms Drew for example admired her hardworking boss and 'the high ups' but thought little of and avoided those whom she referred to as 'the lower orders', thus cutting herself off from potential sources of help. Mrs Dalton gains a personal sense of status at work from for her high grade boss, 'a role model', but not from life outside, in her local community. Describing its bad reputation, she is not enthusiastic about her local environment, and prefers not to mix with locals. Additionally, her job can also be relatively isolating as she has limited contact with people other than her boss. Taken together, her overall isolation meant she was unable to access support outside her family when one of her parents died, for example, and she was very close to depression.

Orientation: Social Relations

For many people whose narratives give prominence to social relations and social support in the workplace, a social relations orientation is one which can encompass their lives entirely. Miss Norden's (AA) story reflects the primacy of social ties in her life and in her perceptions of well-being. She gives a great deal of support, and gains it, from her social networks outside work, while at work itself, she acknowledges that: ‘a good team really matters a lot for me’. Because relationships with her supervisor and the personnel department were poor in her previous post, she found her job very stressful indeed, and gave in her notice. She contrasts the experience with her current job, where she derives much pleasure from getting on very well with her new, and supportive, work colleagues. When one of them visited her when she was in hospital for treatment, she found that: ‘It boosts your morale, and makes you feel that people really do care’.

A function of a social relations orientation for individuals in this context means more than support available or attaining a work/life balance but refers also to the value attached for example to social connections at work and a strong family or community life in supplying needs for happiness, contentment, and companionship. For example, Mrs Andrews’s (AO) social needs were being met in both main domains of her life; as well as having friendly, sociable colleagues her ability to mix with pleasant, helpful neighbours was also crucial for her to feel content and satisfied with life. Getting on with everyone she explained, was central to her outlook. Mrs George’s preferences for sociable and co-operative colleagues and helpful line managers are, as noted earlier, met at work, they are what constitutes a good job for her—feelings typical of many here. Additionally, throughout her interview Mrs George repeatedly refers to the significance to her of her good strong family life, and of her ‘lovely neighbours’. Her thoughts on local life resonate with features we associate with a traditional working-class community. She describes the cul-de-sac where she lives for example as a place where: ‘We know lots of people; you could knock on their door if you were in trouble. And Mum and Dad live just down the [underground] line’. While people in this grade group may identify features which lead them to feeling out of control, for some being *in* control as such is not always readily acknowledged as directly salient. Mrs George responded to questions on personal perceptions of control with reference to the happiness she derives from family life, and the value she places on social ties: ‘Deep down I do like the family life, I’m happy that way. I don’t like being on own, *all my life is fine’*.

Orientation, Experience, and Dissonance

An individual's overall life orientation bears some relationship to what it is they want from life. It follows that where key needs are being met substantially in more than one domain of an individual's life, like some of the examples mentioned above, then he or she will be in a potentially favourable position vis-à-vis their experience of mental health and well-being. Examples additional to some of those already referred to include that of Mrs Sadler (secretary) for example, for whom satisfaction is found both at work and in her neighbourhood. She appreciates working for 'fair people, who value her contribution', while where she lives meets her desire for 'peace and quiet and no-one interfering'. Mrs Vidal (AO) reported that she derives happiness and contentment from all aspects of her life. She appreciates the settled life she has—her job, marriage, place of residence, and her supportive family living nearby. Like many across employment grades, she was attracted to the Civil Service for the security if offered, and enjoys a pleasant atmosphere, a nice office, and people who can be trusted and who are easy to get on with: 'This describes my own job 100%'. Like earlier examples, her local and family life appear to reflect what she values: traditional community life.

When interviewees identify factors which make for an ideal job, or a good home and neighbourhood, and these needs coincide with their experience, then beneficial effects on well-being can be expected; where there is dissonance between orientation and experience, then a stressful outcome appears more likely. Mr Fellowes (CO) always felt unsuited to his job in the Civil Service: 'A most unrewarding job. … I could not be myself, you have to conform to the system'. Referring to a strict security protocol, he said that it did not meet his desire for independence or for control over what he was doing: 'Every time I went to the loo … and at 5.pm every day, you had to pack everything away immediately, and stop right in the middle of a train of thought'. At the same time, he did not wish to have any involvement in his local neighbourhood, which he disliked. Now relocated and self-employed, he gains much from both. He is part of a thriving community, where he enjoys trusting relationships and wide networks, gains satisfaction from a job well done as a builder and craftsman, and feels much more in control than he did before. 'I don't think I was academic enough for office work. Now I've carved a niche for myself, I couldn't feel better about it' (Mr Fellowes, CO). Satisfaction gained from his new life was helping him overcome an inferiority complex which had troubled him since schooldays, and replacing it with a newfound sense of achievement, which, he believed, was an essential requisite, central to his life.

A Vignette

The following case study, though not typical in its entirety, nevertheless usefully illustrates many of the issues discussed in relation to the lower grades group. It concerns Mr Case (AA), a man whose job involved routine support tasks. His narrative suggests acute perceptions of powerlessness on his part—he saw his position as at the bottom rung of the ladder and his job as simply reacting to the needs of others who, he believed, had little understanding of his difficulties. Mr Case gained no job satisfaction from the tasks he performed; the demands of the job were stressful, with more work than he could handle in the time available. He reported that he worked simply as 'a duty' to feed his family.

Amongst other lower grade civil servants also performing routine tasks there were nevertheless many who did not take such a negative view of their work, or indeed of their place in the hierarchy. A difference here was Mr Case's isolation: he worked alone and was not part of a work group, he was unable to make supportive or co-operative connections. What is striking from his account is the extent of his alienation (see Marx, 1844), from the work process, the product of his work, and from his colleagues and management. Blauner's (1964) classic study on alienation argues that a sense of purpose, the degree of control of the work and social integration are important influences, while the meaningfulness of any task, Sayer argued, depends also on employees having an intelligible connection to the larger project to which they belong (Sayer, 2009). In a different, and more sociable, workplace context, a lower grade woman already mentioned, while describing circumstances related to overload in which work can 'make you a bit down … you've got about eight or nine jobs on the go, and sometimes, it just gets on your nerves' (Mrs George), nevertheless intimated that this seemed to be more than cancelled out by good social relations at work, and by the pleasure derived from mixing with colleagues. Others talking in a similar vein included Mrs Yardley for example who is integrated into cohesive work groups of fellow supervisors and of post room staff. What she likes particularly about work is the friendliness and good humour of the work group. Staff enjoy: 'chatting while they work, having a laugh and a joke, listening to the radio'. Enjoying work is what a good job is to her. Further casualisation of this kind of work environment, incidentally, could well be expected to dent the cohesive and co-operative work culture Mrs Yardley was describing.

A second difference between Mr Case and some of his grade equivalents was related to the meaning that his lack of promotion held for him. He had moved to this country as a young man to better himself. There were several cases, like his, of (usually) men, across grades, where negative feelings of frustration and bitterness arising from lack of promotion, are particularly acute where individuals like Mr Case subscribe to a meritocratic ethic, or also, as in his case, believe that they have been discriminated against on grounds of ethnicity. It is little wonder that Mr Case talked about having a 'stress' problem, that work difficulties made him cry, or that he took to drink to forget them. But certain objective conditions, like a lack of promotion, could be invested with different meanings for other individuals. As we have indicated, some people interviewed were quite content with their position in the hierarchy. This was especially the case for some women on lower and middle grades, for whom flexible working arrangements and part time work to suit their family commitments, or pleasant colleagues, were perceived as of more value than career advancement.

A third example of differences between Mr Case and some of his peers, concerns his perceptions of the status of his work: he was unhappy about his place on the bottom of the hierarchy. Rather unexpectedly, given the interest in perceptions of status in the Whitehall II studies and elsewhere (Singh-Manoux et al., 2003), lower grades interviewed for this study appeared to be reasonably accepting of the grade structure (and many had known no other kind of work organisation) and did not feel their work, or themselves, to be inferior in any way to that of those on higher grades. These employees don't compare themselves and their position to the 'high ups'. An example is provided by the case of Mrs Yardley, mentioned earlier, a woman doing a routine job. As well as working enjoyably and co-operatively with a friendly work group and being able to exercise some control over the work process, she was able to interpret her position in a positive light and perceived the job itself as being worthwhile: 'They always say our work is the bottom … but no, if it wasn't for us their work wouldn't go out'. Her sense of humour appears to be an additional coping mechanism for her relatively lowly position in the organisation structure. She joked about 'the old school' of more senior civil servants, who had been accustomed 'to having everything done for them'. Her comments suggest that she felt connected to a wider project, and that she recognised that her work certainly had purpose.

He had been dealt a bad hand at work, yet for Mr Case himself, despair was not evident in all aspects of his life. Negative work experiences were balanced by positive ones outside. Adam Smith (1776) believed that the harmful effects to the mind of boring repetitive work would also damage life outside work, in particular the ability of workers to participate in the life of the community, while more recently, Karasek and Theorell (1990) showed that monotonous work affected people's leisure activities. But Mr Case's experience did not conform to the norm. His family is a source of happiness for him, his neighbourhood a source of contentment, his home—which he owns—a source of prestige, attendance at religious venues provide him with spiritual strength. These are all things he values highly and does not expect his need for them to be met at work. Mr Case's coping strategy in dealing with work problems is to keep the two spheres of work and outside work totally separate, to the extent that he does not talk about his work problems at home, and his social life does not involve anyone from work. The key point here lies in the depth of the value he places in life outside work, thus increasing the efficacy of its potential buffering effect for negatively experienced work characteristics.

Lower Grade Civil Servants: A Summary of Prominent Features

- Lower grades reported experiencing dissatisfaction at work associated with a wide variety of factors including routine; career issues and promotion; communications problems; perceptions of workplace injustice; dysfunctional work units and poor social relations along with difficulties coping with change.
- Poor social relations and conflict, especially with line managers, were a common cause of dissatisfaction and contributed to a sense of injustice.
- A combination of stressors occurring together was experienced as particularly damaging to mental health and well-being.
- Lower grade civil servants overall did not expect to gain much satisfaction from the content of the work.
- Good social relations and positive social ties at work and outside work, of being integrated into a cohesive, co-operative, and

solidaristic work group or community were highly valued. Good working relationships with peers and bosses, as well as contributing directly to the quality of life, helped them cope with problems both at work and at home.

- Changes in the social organisation of the workplace could result in negative effects on job satisfaction and on mental health and well-being.
- Differing individual perspectives and overall life orientations can influence the extent to which work characteristics were experienced and recounted as stressful. They include: a predominant focus on life outside work, actively improving things, status, and social relations.
- Where there is dissonance between orientation and experience, a stressful outcome is more likely.
- The importance of social networks and social support for the lives of individuals in this group was clear. Social support was especially essential at times of stress; lower grades may have had less in the way of other positive entities to fall back on than middle or higher-grade groups. Many spoke principally of close bonding ties, which, though potentially helpful, may be less robust at a time of crisis.

References

Allan, G. (1996). *Kinship and Friendship in Modern Britain.* Oxford University Press.

Blauner, R. (1964). *Alienation and Freedom.* University of Chicago Press.

Cattell, V. (2001). Poor People, Poor Places, and Poor Health: The Mediating Role of Social Networks and Social Capital. *Social Science and Medicine, 52*(10), 1501–1516.

Cattell, V. (2003). Social Networks as Mediators Between the Harsh Circumstances of People's Lives and their Lived Experience of Health and Well-being. In C. Phillipson, G. Allan, & D. Morgan (Eds.), *Social Networks and Social Exclusion: Sociological and Policy Perspectives* (pp. 142–161). Ashgate.

Goldthorpe, J. H., Lockwood, D., Bechhofer, F., & Platt, J. (1968). *The Affluent Worker: Industrial Attitudes and Behaviour.* Cambridge University Press.

Independent Age. (2014). *Isolation: The Emerging Crisis for Older Men.* Independent Age.

Karasek, R. A. and Theorell, T. (1990). *Healthy Work: Stress, Productivity and the Reconstruction of Working Life.* Basic Books.

Layard, R. (2005). *Happiness, Penguin.* Books: London.

Marx. (1844/1988). *The Economic and Philosophical Manuscripts* (M. Milligan, Trans.). Prometheus Books.

Pearlin, L. I. (1989). The Sociological Study of Stress. *Journal of Health and Social Behaviour, 30*, 241–256.

Sayer, A. (2009). Contributive justice and meaningful work'. *Res Publica, 15*(1), 1–16.

Sayer, A. (2011). *Why Things Matter to People: Social Science, Values and Ethical Life*. Cambridge University Press.

Singh-Manoux, A., Adler, N. E., & Marmot, M. G. (2003). Subjective Social Status: Its Determinants and Its Association with Measures of Ill-health in the Whitehall II Study. *Social Science and Medicine, 56*, 1321–1333.

Smith, A. (1776). *The Wealth of Nations.* W Strahan and T Cadell.

CHAPTER 3

Middle Grades: Co-Operation, Participation, and Work-Life Balance

Abstract Middle grade civil servants were able to pinpoint their enjoyment of specific work tasks. Working structures which encourage teamwork and co-operative working arrangements are appreciated as is an understanding for some that their work is of value for example. Dissatisfactions at work included: staffing structures experienced as too many bosses; a high departmental workload; cuts and the damage to services; structural changes; problems with performance appraisal; insufficient promotion chances; and poor social relations with colleagues or supervisors. Many dislike workplace change; some believe that experience is valued less than it once was. Mitigating features can include those aspects of work from which they gain satisfaction. Along with coping strategies, additional issues raised concern about the particular context; valued work; social support, co-operation, and collective action; and leading a balanced life. Involvement in outside activities and through this achieving a work-life balance was an especially prominent feature of this middle grade group, something valued highly by respondents and understood by them as beneficial to their psychological health.

Keywords Work-life balance • Participation • Well-being • Cuts • Professional • Security • Co-operation • Re-organisation • Promotion • Pride

V. Cattell, S. Stansfeld, *Work in the Balance*,
https://doi.org/10.1007/978-3-031-96582-1_3

In this chapter we examine the lives and experiences of middle grade civil servants, that is, Executive Officers (EO), Higher Executive Officers (HEO), and Senior Executive Officers (SEO). As in Chap. 2, we look at aspects of work and life outside which were found to be satisfying and fulfilling by respondents or problematic and stressful, and identify factors which ameliorated or exacerbated stressful experience. Meanings invested in these various elements are considered.

It can be useful to see grade differences as occurring not wholly between grade groups, but as a continuum. For example, a few individuals at the EO end of the middle grade range—such as one who preferred the routine, familiarity, and enjoyable social aspects of the job he experienced before he was promoted into the middle ranks—could have more in common with clerical and support grades than with their own more senior colleagues, while some of those at the higher end of the middle grades spectrum may share features with those found on the lower rungs of higher grades.

Some factors associated with the context of their working lives can be noted. Middle grade civil servants lived in a range of different housing types, both rented and owner occupied, and typically on the outskirts of London. Living in social housing was not common for this group and feeling settled in their area of residence appeared less common than for many on higher grades buying their homes. It can take longer for some people on modest incomes, for example, to settle in a place they feel happy in than it does for many of those on higher incomes, something which carries implications for community life. An EO reported for example that he will aim for promotion eventually, so that he will be able to afford to move to a 'nicer area', with less crime and other problems, and where 'people take pride in their property'.

Gaining Satisfaction at Work

Certain individuals were attracted to the security the Civil Service offered and appreciated having a regular salary to pay the mortgage, but extrinsic aspects of the job like this were mentioned less regularly than expected. Some however may have just considered issues like these as taken for granted, too usual to be remarked upon. When speaking of aspects of their employment which they found enjoyable, middle grades, in contrast to their lower grade colleagues, tended to focus on aspects of the job content, highlighting specific work tasks. For example, some gained satisfaction from writing answers to Parliamentary Questions, from dealing with departmental correspondence or responding to enquiries from the public. Additional work characteristics appreciated and mentioned by several included having a clear, well-defined job with discrete boundaries.

Middle grade civil servants in the study, especially those at HEO and SEO levels, tend to eschew routine and were more likely to prefer a certain amount of interesting and challenging work. Mr Yarham (HEO), for example, enjoys his job because: 'it's demanding enough not to get too boring', sentiments which become more pronounced as seniority progresses. Mr Nichol (SEO), a man who is highly knowledgeable about his own work and that of his department, relishes problem solving and challenges, as does Mr Ivens (HEO), who, alluding to perceptions of control, not only appreciates having a well-defined job, that is: 'having a block of work that you can manage yourself from start to finish', but also finds it 'satisfying if you can solve the problem by the time the file leaves you'. While being able to complete a task was found gratifying, there was also a sense however amongst some middle grade civil servants that they took comfort in knowing that they did not have to take overall responsibility for the entire project.

Though less widespread than among higher grades, some middle grade individuals are motivated by and gain satisfaction from an understanding of their role as underpinned by a public service ethic (see later), or from a recognition, on the part of others or themselves, that the work they do is valuable and important. Mr Silva (HEO), who was finding aspects of his current job stressful, considered his most enjoyable job to be 'when I was doing something useful, and I was valued'. Mr Ivens (HEO) very much enjoyed working on tasks at a time of international crisis: 'If you have one major overriding objective … it's much less stressful than coping with lots of little things'. Similarly, Mr Nichol (HEO) talked about the essential work he and his department are doing—continuously in this case—to protect government services and public utilities during an emergency or a disaster, work he recognised as highly critical for the efficacy of the public sector.

Social Relations and Co-operation

There were some similarities, but also differences, in the ways in which middle grades, in comparison with lower grades, refer to social interaction and positive social relations as enjoyable aspects of their working lives.

Rather than talking about social relations or departmental cultures in general terms, some mentioned specific job holders or their section structure favourably in this context. For Mr Silva (HEO) a man who appreciates predictability and order, it is important that he gets on with the person reporting to him and the person he reports to. Mr Mason (EO) benefits from having something in common with his (largely male) colleagues and takes pleasure from the sense of humour which he attributes to the man he sits next to and the person he reports to.

Good social relations in the form of co-operative work practices, along with teamwork and their enabling structures, are generally viewed positively by this group. Co-operation and a cohesive environment are experienced as workplace features which reduce stress for men and women on this grade. For example: 'Cross work discussion is supportive', opined one, or can be empowering vis-à-vis management, reported another. Some identified conditions under which teamwork and co-operation is engendered or undermined. Those which encourage co-operation include stability of the departmental, branch or sectional staffing, relatively flat organisation structures made up of teams of similar grades, or more traditional section structures which, though still hierarchal, were perceived as egalitarian because bosses worked closely with their subordinates. In some contexts, the nature of the work, such as that involving sections (a work unit) made up of professional engineers, made co-operation an essential aspect of the job. Features of the workplace having favourable effects on co-operation also included those which help build trust. Mr Mason (EO) believed that a good sense of humour amongst his colleagues helps to build up trust, something which in turn, underpins co-operative behaviour. For Mrs Essen (EO) colleagues getting together in the pub on Fridays had positive benefits in this respect.

A quite different promoter of co-operation was evident at a time of international crisis, mentioned earlier, and described by Mr Ivens (HEO) as a time when people readily bonded together to get essential work done. Additional, more mundane factors with a role to play include the office layout, proximity of facilities like tea points etc., or the physical location of the department. Mr Ivens (HEO) contrasted London offices with his current post located in a countryside setting outside London. Physical isolation, he observed, strengthens sociability and solidarity, as does the employment of local people on clerical grades, and staff arriving and leaving at the same time. As a consequence, more people, he said, would turn up for social occasions or would be active in the union than would be expected in London. The example is unusual, given that the majority of civil servants taking part in the study travel into central London to work; these aspects of his workplace which he described resonate with features we associate with the development of strong 'community' life.

One of the downsides to re-organisation—in the direction of more team working and flatter structures and mentioned by several in the middle grades—was that more demands were made of people, and more expected of them. Being overloaded has implications for the efficacy and benefits of teamwork and co-operation. For Mr Farmer (HEO), staff cutbacks, which can be a feature of re-organisation, have resulted in an increased workload, which in turn has implemented a reduction in co-operation amongst staff in his unit. Time constraints mean that: 'No one has time to do things for others anymore'. Intensification in the workplace can have a detrimental effect on the trusting relationships necessary for co-operation and the development of social capital. A higher grade woman, talking about civil servants as a whole, reported that people trust, consult, and co-operate with colleagues less when work levels are high, simply because, under pressure, they are less likely to tell each other what they are doing. Too sudden changes to how things are done, new grade marking and the nature of staff reporting systems could also have negative effects on co-operative working relations. An HEO reported that: 'We were all working as a team, then a new boss comes along and tries to change the system immediately. Another observed that staff jealousies could break out as a result of a new grade marking system linked to salaries while an SEO, Mr Nichol, focused instead on how new systems were implemented: 'Personnel handled the new reporting system very poorly leaving a lot of people dissatisfied and less willing to co-operate as a result'.

Dissatisfaction and Well-Being

Dissatisfactions at work raised by middle grades were various and included matters associated with task variety; staffing structures; a high departmental workload; cuts and the damage to services; structural changes; performance appraisal; promotion chances; and poor social relations with colleagues or supervisors.

Overload

Experiencing a certain amount of variety can be generally appreciated, but Mr Mason's (EO) case illustrates how variety in work tasks can be onerous if there is too much of it. He had transferred to a new job two weeks before he was interviewed. Describing his previous post, he said that his own work there had been much too diffuse. The structure of the unit, in particular the large number of people he reported to was a problem for him, not least for his sense of control. Alluding to the high level of demands made on him, he said: 'I was the only non-specialist in a large busy section; I had too many bosses. It was difficult to meet all the deadlines, I was at everyone's beck and call and had to constantly re-prioritise. I never felt in control of the job, and I felt guilty when I couldn't meet all the deadlines they wanted and blamed myself for not being good enough, or fast enough' (Mr Mason, EO).

Increased work pressure and a heavy workload were quite common complaints. A combination of increased work and changes to working practices resulted in too few people doing too much work observed Mr Silva (HEO). Experiencing an expansion in responsibilities was seen as having various negative effects on job satisfaction. For Mr Innes (HEO) for example, a key downside to his job concerned the: 'many new initiatives coming from above leaving you with not enough time to do what you want to do'. Along with the reduction in co-operation amongst staff already mentioned, Mr Donaldson (HEO) drew attention to some additional effects of cuts and which for him, were a major source of dissatisfaction at work: 'Reduction in staff and resources means we are not able to provide the *quality of work* [our ital.] which we once did. At the same time, the volume of correspondence I deal with has rocketed'. He believes that his current boss does not do enough to defend his department from cutbacks. Unusually, and in contrast to these examples, it is an insufficient workload which is seen as a potential difficulty by one senior middle grade. Mr Nichol (SEO), a man who relishes the problems and challenges which are a built-in feature of his job said: 'When everything goes smoothly, and there is very little to do, that's the worst time actually, being underutilised'. Reflecting a fear of job loss, he added: 'My only work-related worry is whether there is likely to be sufficient work to make the job worthwhile'.

Experiencing Change

Structural change at work can sometimes be a stressful experience. Examples include Human Resources (HR) taking over control of an area of work previously dealt with within the department (Mr Farmer HEO), or the reconfiguration of responsibility for specific job tasks within a unit. Mr Ivens (HEO), whilst acknowledging that such changes can produce gains in efficiency, also recognised an important disbenefit connected to people's sense of ownership of the job: 'People can't take pride in their own little job anymore, you have to be part of a big structure, and this tends to have an effect on morale'.

Grade marking, mandatory annual reporting, and performance related pay were recognised by higher grade civil servants as problems for their middle grade colleagues especially. Being paid by skill level and not grade along with a lack of transparency was causing problems among staff and damaging co-operative practices. People were said to be less willing to do work which does not feature in their job description for example. Changes in pay structures were identified by a higher grade woman as reflecting a tendency in the service to value experience much less than it once did. Amongst middle grades themselves, changes to the system of performance appraisal were seen as highly problematic and could be experienced as demoralising for some, especially those on the more junior end of the middle grade spectrum. In some cases, such as that of Mr Ivens (HEO), dislike of the system not only sprung from being judged on his performance, which was stressful in itself, but also from being at the receiving end of staff complaints. They blamed him for not being better appraised themselves, thus: 'Judgement was coming from above and below'. He added also that the system could be damaging to good social relations, that staff jealousies could break out. Mrs Lawson, a higher grade woman, commenting on performance appraisal and its effects across grades, middle grades especially, recognised that the reporting system can be made to work if managers treat it positively, by making appropriate suggestions for example, rather than negative comments.

Several were unhappy with changes to the way the promotion system operated. Mr Innes (HEO), for example felt that the certainty of career progression had gone. Linking this to changed approaches to valuing experience, he said: 'Promotion is now competitive based instead of experience based. Any experience you may have built up is totally disregarded'. He saw this as unfair and unjust, and felt powerless to improve his own chances. Mr Innes felt under stress when he was required to write an application for promotion—something he had not had to do before—because 'I had no idea how to write it or what they were looking for'. Generally, he feels in control of work tasks and believes himself to be competent and experienced; people regularly ask him for information, and he is able to provide it. However, not having the necessary writing skills to complete an application satisfactorily led him to feel out of control of the situation. Taking a balanced view, another HEO, Mr. Ivens, explained: 'The old promotion board system had its weaknesses, some people would fall through net, others promoted above their capabilities. When the system changed, you had to apply for particular jobs, and were judged on suitability for that post. It's a mixed thing, but I do think that managers themselves should be more involved in selection for promotion'.

Social Relations at Work, Relations with Peers and Superiors

Along with perceived shortcomings generally related to a lack of support or communication issues, problems middle grade civil servants experienced with superiors also centred on management style. A few described theirs as too controlling or overly critical, something which could damage their self-confidence or awareness of being in control of the work. Mrs Dyce (EO), who had recently changed posts, described her new manager as 'a control freak. Nothing is ever good enough; there is never a word of praise'. Mr Fenton (EO)—who was very distressed in his new supervisory role—also expressed misgivings about his new line manager, who, unlike the previous post holder, does not listen or suggest ways to solve problems. Poor communications with his line manager took a different form for Mr Silva (HEO), who gets sent 'to meetings when I'm not properly informed, and don't know what the department line is', a bewildering situation which he finds very stressful indeed.

Though not a regular occurrence amongst this group of civil servants, Ms Benson (HEO) provides an example of the distress caused when relations with colleagues go badly wrong. A situation arose in which she was bullied left her feeling anxious, vulnerable and out of control. Because the person allegedly bullying her 'took control of the situation, running around telling everyone socially that I was [something she strongly denies and does not understand] … and it got back to my staff', she was left feeling powerless. These feelings were exacerbated because she was unable to confide in or gain support from her line manager, and because of a long delay before the manager took action. The line manager herself however may have had difficulties in accessing guidance on the very difficult identity issues involved. A civil servant in another department, who recognised the benefits to improved social relations of the greater emphasis being placed on training in the Service mentioned that: 'As well as gaining more knowledge about doing their jobs effectively people have been trained in dealing with colleagues. It has made them more conscious of how they react to other people'.

A Co-incidence of Stressors

Damaging outcomes connected to a range of difficulties occurring simultaneously were experienced by people across all three grade groups. Middle grade examples include that of Mrs Dyce, recently promoted to EO, for whom a co-incidence of stressors involving work and home life and an absence of support in both took a toll on her health. She was responsible for looking after her sick, elderly mother, her unemployed husband was ill, and she cared for her grandchild at the weekends. At work she changed posts, where she felt, and was made to feel by others, that she was performing badly. She received little training for her new duties however: 'You're just plonked into work and have to get on with it, you are not given any training', and continues to feel anxious about aspects of the job she does not feel competent in doing without help. She added: 'So I think that all added to the pressure that I was already under with my mum and my husband'. Low financial resources exacerbate her problems. In a context of additional worry caused by her husband 'spending too much money' and receiving a letter detailing the need for unexpected and expensive repairs to their house—a former council property—money problems emerged as a trigger for depression. She was ashamed of how she felt and blamed herself: 'Although I am a worrier, I'm usually quite good at taking pressure. But I felt so awful that I was giving in, that I couldn't handle it. I think that made it worse because I thought that I was being weak. I didn't want to get out of the bed, and just kept crying. … I felt safe in there. I couldn't face the thought of getting ready and walking out of the door. And I kept having thoughts, in my mind you know like, "what is the point of it all"' (Mrs Dyce EO).

Intervening Factors: Protecting Well-Being, Minimising, Or Driving Stress

Whilst middle grades may have been subject to a range of problems at work and for some, outside as well, the many positive aspects of their everyday lives they identified were able to help lessen their deleterious effects. Mitigating features, for example, can include those aspects of work from which they gain satisfaction. Along with coping strategies, issues raised additional to gaining satisfaction from other aspects of the job concerned, for example, the particular context; valued work; social support, co-operation and collective action; leading a balanced life plus certain individual attitudes or personality factors.

In certain contexts, problems like overload, or departmental downsizing, appeared less likely to be recounted as stressful. Mr Yarham (HEO), who is very positive about his work group, provides an example of a section working well. He reported that although a downsizing exercise in the department was handled badly and created bad feeling amongst staff generally, his own unit nevertheless weathered the storm. A combination of an approachable boss, nice colleagues, co-operative working relations, and a helpful and social work group appeared to enable the section to handle change and potentially stressful conditions. He talks to his line manager and the section head everyday about work, for example, both of whom he finds helpful. It should be noted perhaps that his is not a typical section structure, they are all, apart from the head (grade 6), on executive employment grades.

Middle grades were also able to cope with extra demands made on them when they perceived their work to be highly valuable, as was noted earlier in the context of an international crisis. Mr Ivens (HEO) added for example that: 'People were happy to work long hours [at this time], because they recognised the work was important … so it was not a stressful time'. Additional factors which can mitigate negatively perceived work characteristics—such as overload or lack of promotion for example—are not simply related to the particular work context but include those which could be invested with different meanings for individuals. Some of those interviewed were quite content with their position in the hierarchy, and not interested in developing their careers further. As with lower grades, this was especially the case for some women on middle grades, for whom flexible working arrangements and part time work to suit their family commitments, and/or pleasant colleagues, were understood as of more value than career advancement. Included in this group were also men and women at the lower end of the grade group who, having experienced a stress related illness or episode in the past, wanted to avoid what they perceived as the anxiety laden added burden of more responsibility or the longer hours which they associated with promotion.

Some civil servants who intimated that they were feeling low when interviewed were not interested in promotion for different reasons, ones which they identified as relating to their own perceived shortcomings, or a decline in confidence in their own abilities, as well as a fear of being overburdened. A co-incidence of stressors in the form of an overload of responsibilities at home and a new post at work, and her consequent depression, appeared to have changed Mrs Dyce's attitudes to applying for promotion: 'I was interested in getting promotion at one time, but I just don't have it in me anymore. My interviewing skills are probably not good enough anyway. I've lost a lot of confidence; when I was younger, I felt very confident, and never had any problems with jobs'. While not finding satisfaction at work can negatively affect mental health and well-being, Mrs Dyce's case illustrates how the relationship can also work in the reverse direction, low mood itself hampering her ability to gain satisfaction at work. The only time she enjoyed her tasks, she acknowledged, was she had finished them: 'when I've got through something I particularly don't enjoy doing'.

In contrast, factors ameliorating work problems like a lack of promotion and their stress promoting effects also include the ability to gain satisfaction from other aspects of the job, or from the work as a whole, or from outside activities. For example, despite some disappointment at not having risen further in the ranks, Mr Farmer (HEO) is nevertheless happy in his work, very much enjoys it, and knows that it is valued. At the same time, he has gained national status and recognition through his charitable activities outside the workplace. For another HEO, who recently 'came out', having sufficient time to spend with his new partner and on his music were now taking prominence in his life, and he is no longer interested in further promotion.

Coping with Difficult and Stressful Situations

Amongst aspects of everyday life which helped middle grades taking part in the study to cope with difficult and negatively experienced situations were those connected to receiving social support, co-operative work practices, possessing a religious faith, and living a balanced life. Individual personality and the meanings associated with work experiences also had roles to play, as did their overall life orientations.

Support

Male civil servants especially spoke of gaining emotional support from their partners. Mr Silva (HEO), for example, relies heavily on his girlfriend and trusts her completely. She is able to calm him down when he feels enraged at things going wrong at work. While many, male and female, recognise that being able to meet friends and share emotional and practical problems with them has a beneficial effect on their well-being, not all of the male civil servants in this group look on friends as a source of emotional support. Mr Long (SEO) indicated that while he has few friends, he does not consider this to be a problem as he strongly believes that he does not need support, preferring instead to rely on himself. Yet in another case, and despite a fairly busy social life involving many friends, Mr Mason (EO) felt unable to talk to men friends about emotional problems or seek support from them. When in his last post, there was no one available to relate to about difficulties in a job in which he felt very dissatisfied. As a younger man, he would drink to mask feelings of suffering. Referring to how he used to feel until quite recently he said: 'I always felt, "what's the point"'. I often had that depressed, empty feeling. Even when things were going right, I didn't have any enthusiasm'. Now, a supportive and sympathetic girlfriend, along with finding a new (for him) religion and moving to a new civil service post much more suited to his needs for more control over his work and fewer bosses, mean that his well-being is improving. Mr Mason is overcoming a lack of confidence which he believed stemmed from an unhappy childhood which involved attendance at a very strict religious school and at times difficult relationships with his parents and is developing a strengthened resilience: 'I don't get so depressed and melancholy now. I count my blessings and feel more content. I'm not being affected so much when things go wrong'. The damaging effects of multiple problems, some quite long term, in his case were overcome through a changed job context and plentiful supports both inside and outside the workplace.

In contrast to cases like these, we found examples of people unable to access help when in need. Mr Fenton (EO) is unhappy at work. As well as finding his new line manager unsupportive, he feels unable to seek help from his wife as she has depression too: 'She worries about me and I about her and I worry about her worrying about me so it all builds up'. Mrs Dyce (EO) received startlingly little help in dealing with her many problems. She had suffered from depression in the year prior to interview and remained on medication. A co-incidence of stressors involving work and home life and an absence of support in both took a toll on her mental health. She detailed her lack of assistance at home: 'All the family responsibility is on my shoulders, "Mum will sort it out" they say. My brothers were content to let me get on with everything when I was looking after my mother ... my husband was not supportive when I was depressed, he's embarrassed by it, and doesn't know how to deal with it'. Taken together, a plethora of stressors she was unable to share with others left Mrs Dyce with an awareness of little control over her life: 'I'm coming out to work and just existing and life is just slipping away. ... You don't have a choice really because you've got all of these commitments'. A sense of alienation from work and home comes across strongly in her case. She no longer expected to find self-fulfilment in either domain. A sole source of social respite from her current problems appeared to be her Sunday visits to the residents' social club on her housing estate, where she finds it 'helpful just to go there and chat'.

A second case illustrative of some of the potential perils to mental health and well-being of giving more support than one feels equal to comes from Mr Nichol (SEO), a man who derives a great deal of enjoyment from his work and recognises it as highly valuable. Yet Mr Nichol nevertheless was suffering from what appeared to be a form of burnout, not as a result of his own workload, but because of the amount of assistance he was giving his wife in running her business. He explained: 'She always takes on too much work ... evenings and weekends are stressful and difficult to manage'. He feels overstretched, has regular flu like symptoms, does not get enough sleep and has no time for the activities and hobbies which he used to enjoy. He feels under stress when trying to fit his own and his wife's work together and finds any additional family problems that come along very difficult to tackle and wearisome. He links his perceptions of lack of control with his inability to achieve his goal of more free time at weekends and in the evenings.

Co-operation

Co-operative social relations in the workplace, as already mentioned, are valued by middle grade civil servants and seen as helpful when learning new tasks or facing difficulties, or as productive vis-à-vis management. A woman described how people in her department coped collectively with work problems and changes for example: 'We haven't let them get away with a too gung-ho approach to changing things, we are an assertive lot, we don't just suffer in silence'. Mrs Warren (SEO) was describing a situation in which a sense of individual and collective agency could be strengthened. Referring to her departmental culture which encourages participation in decision-making and where 'it's okay for people at relatively junior levels to speak out and say their piece she added: 'it empowers you'.

An engineer, Mr Orford (HEO) reported that he and his colleagues were able to withstand the stress associated with the many changes to the job following re-organisation, essentially because the social organisation peculiar to the team—co-operative work practices and the stability needed to ensure them—went unchanged. Their loss of the supportive backups at their disposal until recently—certain management structures, libraries, technical assistance, and further training—meant that they had to rely even more on their colleagues to cope. Despite having to take on board new ideas and new ways of working, and in some cases becoming physically ill (this informant developed an ulcer), Mr Orford said that his work unit did not appear to suffer adverse effects on their mental health at the time: 'You are all in the same boat … we were all being clobbered, you know, so it was all backs to the wall. And this is where you get a lot of strength from your colleagues'. His experience emphasises the positive strength and importance of peer co-operation when other forms of assistance are not available. He was now concerned however that the trend to employing increasing numbers of agency staff would destroy co-operative working practices.

Faith, Participation, and a Work/Life Balance

Both men and women in middle grades access emotional and practical support and advice from friends and acquaintances made through their place of worship. Mr Innes (HEO) for example, who lives in a commuter area with little neighbourly sense of community, regards his church as his community, members of which he can ask for support and advice when necessary. Just as frequently however, interviewees expressed the importance of their religious faith itself in helping them cope with problems. Mr Innes's belief in God enables him 'to leave any problems with Him; [then] I can switch off from work problems'. Mr Innes does not look back at the past, or worry about the future, but 'takes each day as it comes', a phrase he uses not only in relation to stress, but which he also connects to helping him feel in control of his life. Ms Benson's (HEO) faith is helping her to take control over the difficulties she experienced. She is convinced that: 'Faith gives one purpose of character. I have gained tremendous insights by praying. I could have let the bitterness [resulting from serious interpersonal work problems] fester but I realised that I must not let this happen and behave differently'. Mr Donaldson (HEO) is one who derives both direct and indirect benefits from religious belief. He maintains that a strong faith provides a firm framework to fit his life around; a very firm view of life both promotes his mental well-being and helps him cope with problems: 'And certainly my faith means that when inevitably there are disappointments, difficulties in life, one can put it in perspective and the problem shouldn't be tipping you over the edge'.

Participation in religious activities is one of several forms of engagement mentioned by interviewees which can be seen to allow a more balanced life to be achieved than where the sole or major focus is on work. Ms Benson (HEO) copes with the difficult situation in her department not only through her religious faith and regular support from friends with whom she can share her problems, but also by ensuring that, as a single woman, she leads a full life outside work. Living in an area with a strong culture of participation, she is very active in her local community, and stressed the direct benefits of involvement, finding it sociable and enjoyable: 'I don't want to go home after work and just watch tv'. Similarly, Mr Farmer (HEO), a man who takes part in many local and national organisations and charities leads a highly active life. Participation not only widens his networks beneficially, for example: 'contacts are very useful for information and solving problems', but, Mr Farmer recognises, also keeps him fit and mentally alert. For these examples, and the next, the achievement of a balanced life is a principal goal in life.

Mr Donaldson (HEO), who provided a very detailed and informed account of both his workplace and the social organisation of his neighbourhood, lives in a middle class area which has a robust sense of community feeling, associated here with unusually high levels of participation in voluntary organisations. He is himself heavily involved in local organisations and campaigns, often as chair or secretary of committees, and takes part regularly in charity work through a national religious organisation. For some people, difficulties in one area of life can impinge on another, but, rather like the example of Mr Case, discussed in Chap. 2, he does not let this happen: 'Certainly at the moment there is a considerable degree of stress at work, and I am not immune from that, but you know, I refuse to take my work problems home or bring my home problems to work. I think that that is probably is helpful [for mental health and well-being]'. As well as helping him to cope with life's problems, Mr Donaldson also gains direct satisfaction and fulfilment from all his activities. Taking an Aristotelian perspective perhaps, he believes that pleasure is a component of doing something, that it cannot be sought in itself. We could surmise that a strong commitment to his outside activities would probably make it less likely that he would allow work problems to impinge on them.

Personality and Attitudes

An individual's personality, such as a determination to overcome difficulty, or the adoption of a realistic attitude, were also seen to affect the extent to which problems were experienced as stressful. Mrs Essen for example reported that she always felt that she could take control of a situation: 'Even if there's a problem, I know I can resolve it. There's no way I would let myself go. I'll stay awake all night, you know, and make sure that I deal with it to my satisfaction. ... I'm not one of those who ever get depressed in my life, No, I'm a hundred percent positive. I'm very much in control and I don't think there's anything I couldn't handle in my own life'.

Those middle grades with a rational approach to life and its difficulties were interesting here. Mr Donaldson (HEO), for example, expressed a thoughtful consideration of his life and working experience and any difficulties he encounters. He believes that a considered and realistic approach protects him from worrying and stress, and, unusually for those taking part in our study, and quite possibly a wider demographic too, sees little point in worrying about wanting something which is not possible to achieve, whether at work or in his personal life. 'So, on the whole' he confided, 'I would say I am not a worrier. I'm fairly philosophical about situations. I can certainly get very impatient and sometimes this will lead me to unwise decisions or activities or whatever. But by and large I think that I can cope with most things, because I can put them in perspective and appreciate what can be done and what can't be done. I am not one to waste time pursuing something which I realise is a lost cause to start with. ... I have simply not wasted energy and emotional energy as well on something which I didn't think I was in a position to do anything about'.

Another example in this vein concerns Mr Ivens (HEO), who took an even handed, measured approach when responding to questions, and displayed a high degree of self-knowledge. When referring to negative aspects of work, he usually identified a positive side of what he is describing as well. For example, when talking of workplace changes: 'Sometimes you lose some control over certain things. ... My own job became more impersonal, and I got less satisfaction at the end'. He acknowledges however that certain changes can produce gains in efficiency. Additionally, though disappointed by his lack of promotion, Mr Ivens does not entirely blame others, or the system, but acknowledges that there were things that he might have done differently. For example: 'I'm quite reliable on the job but failed to originate ideas'. Similarly, Mr Donaldson (HEO) expressed some dissatisfaction that promotion had eluded him but recognises that a reason: 'may be a personality thing, I don't always get on with people'. We could suppose that these reactions and understandings may be more beneficial approaches when it comes to effects on well-being, through feelings of control for example, than laying all blame either on oneself or on the system at work. Mr Long (SEO) for example, blamed himself entirely for making some wrong work-related decisions and when interviewed reported that he was suffering from anxiety and low mood and was feeling out of control.

Meanings and Orientations

If problems occur or changes take place which relate to aspects of work which carry a particularly strong and positive meaning for the individual concerned, then the effects can be frustrating, demoralising, and for some, especially upsetting and damaging to their well-being. Orientations, that is, especially strong meanings, emerging from interviews with middle grade civil servants, whilst including the importance to them of characteristics like job security and career progression, would often relate to more intrinsic work features such as a need for order and predictability or for co-operative relations among staff, or instead were linked to their personal values such as self-reliance, subscription to a public service ethic, and professional pride. For some, as already noted, the achievement of a work/life balance is paramount.

Security, Order, and Predictability

An expectation of a secure job is one of the reasons why these public sector workers join the Service. Referring to changes in the way the promotion system operates, Mr Innes (HEO) felt that the certainty of career progression and job security, which were important to him and some of his colleagues, had gone: 'When I joined the Civil Service, I knew what was expected of me, and then you find, halfway through, that it has totally changed. The Civil Service will become like private industry ... but there's a group of people who want a good, secure job, including myself, [and who are worried]. You need a good job to pay the mortgage. Weber's (Gerth and Mills, 1970) identification of a bureaucratic model as a system of rigid rules, a sense of (Javert-like) fear, perhaps, of disintegration of the old order is also reflected in Mr Silva's case. He had done well, achieving the grade of HEO having joined the Civil Service at 16 as a clerical assistant. He acknowledged a strong desire on his part for a sense of order and predictability of everyday activities. When these are threatened, he panics, and fears he is losing control. Changes in the direction of increasing work, but more especially, to established and familiar work practices, for example, 'I just can't keep up with the new [financial] ranges I deal with', result in him feeling threatened, or angry. Changes in the direction of less autonomy also appear particularly irksome: 'So many changes are going on, and the old rules are changing. When this happens, you can end up with hotchpotch of different rules being applied. For someone who likes to have some sense of order over things, it's very frustrating' (Mr Silva, HEO). In his case, his needs are not being met at work or at home, recently separated from his wife, he continued: 'Home? I don't feel in control there either. I feel I must do these things, like take my son to football at weekends or visit my elderly mother'. When things go wrong at work, which he says is most of the time, he becomes enraged. Describing his current state of mind Mr Silva said: 'I seem to be under stress most of the time, you know both in work and out of work. I'm always watching the clock. ... I must get things done so I can get onto the next thing. That's for everything I do'. His GHQ response indicates that he sees himself playing a useful part, or as capable of making decisions, less than usual, and feels more than usually under strain, finds life a struggle, is panicky, and losing confidence.

Reliance on Self and Need for Control

Mr Long's (SEO) overall orientation to life is centred on a belief in self-reliance and a need for control. He feels that he does not need support, preferring to rely on himself: 'If things happen which we don't like, then we haven't controlled the situation properly'. He had left the Civil Service because he was not promoted, then made some 'unwise investments' and now blames himself for making the wrong decisions: 'It's the worst decision I ever made; It's very hard to forgive myself for it'. His own self-esteem depended on his being able to support his wife and children financially: 'I was determined that I would be able to do that'. He felt unsuccessful for a man of his age: 'I could kick myself for being so stupid as to not have done more with my life'. Though now in another job, Mr Long is not happy there, feels insecure, and remains feeling down, anxious, and not in control.

Good Social Relations

Good social relations are important for people in both lower and middle grades. Work relationships, in the form of co-operation, and people getting on well together feature highly in what Mr Fenton (EO), who, as noted earlier feels he has much in common with the lower grade colleagues he used to operate alongside, prioritises for job satisfaction. It is work which appears central to his life—his friendships tends to be made at the workplace, and not outside. But work is not meeting his needs. When interviewed, he had just taken 7 weeks off for depression and anxiety and has been taking medication for 6 months. He explained that he very much preferred the routine, familiarity, and comradeship he experienced before he was promoted from a lower grade post, and would have been happier, he says, if he had remained where he was, working in tandem with the people he now supervised. Additionally, he recognised a tendency to keep his own emotions under wraps: 'I can get very annoyed inside but don't like to show it. If the deliveries were late, I just say fair enough, whereas other managers would get angry and shout at them. People say I'm too easy going, but I'd rather everybody would be friends and just get on with it'. Responding to a question on perceptions of control he said: 'I prefer to get the people you work with onside. I don't like being domineering. I prefer to discuss things with them'. But, he added, he was finding this more difficult now with instructions coming 'straight down the line, so we

[EOs and HEOs] have learnt to keep problems to ourselves'. A change for the worse in social relations in his unit, when a member of staff was refusing to co-operate, emerged as a tipping point for Mr Fenton's emotional health. A young woman habitually took sick leave immediately following holiday leave and did not get in on time in the mornings: 'It was causing friction amongst the staff, so I was getting their concerns and worries too. And she wouldn't talk to them either. Yet it's always been a very friendly pool of staff. ... I was worried this morning. When I came in, I breathed a sigh of relief because she wasn't there'.

Public Service Ethic and Professional Pride

Although a slightly less widespread motivation than amongst higher grades, some middle grade civil servants are attracted to the Service for reasons connected to a public service ethic and gain satisfaction from a belief in the high quality of their work or from being able to make a positive difference to the lives of others. As Mr Mason (EO), for example, expressed it: 'I think people should be encouraged to see themselves as part of society, contribute to society, and make it a better place for everyone rather than just their section of society or their own individual needs', values which we might expect may be more likely to be shared in the public sector than in some others.

Mr Donaldson (HEO) combines a strong orientation to public service with a strong sense of professional pride: 'I have a fierce belief in doing everything as well as I can'. He places a high value on his work, where he takes pride in the achievements of his department. When interviewed, his very conscientiousness was being threatened; however, cuts, reductions in staff and resources, plus simultaneously expanding departmental work remits, mean that he and his colleagues are not able to produce the quality of work which they once did: 'To see degeneration of the service is dispiriting. This damages pride and morale. It is very frustrating to do less than one is capable of for reasons beyond my control. I had to relinquish a valued research project for example because there was no possibility of getting it done in the time scale. Nonetheless, for reasons outlined earlier, for example, a work/life balance, religious faith, and a rational approach to problems, Mr Donaldson's own mental health was not seemingly adversely affected. We could conjecture perhaps that a typical higher grade officer in a similar situation would probably have continued with the research project and accepted that his/her life outside would suffer, but

Mr Donaldson's pivotal orientation to achieving a balanced life, and with it the high value he places on his voluntary activities as well as his work indicate that, as he acknowledges himself, he would not let that happen.

A striking example of the benefits to be derived from a very full life concerns an HEO whose strong desire for service to others and improving people's lives, are needs which are met in both main arenas of his life. Mr Farmer is highly altruistic, devoting his life to others, even to the extent of using his annual leave to volunteer to help those he sees as less fortunate than himself. His commitment to participation in voluntary associations, local tenants' groups and campaigns, and national charities, as well as to his civil service job which entails arranging social and sports activities and which he believes give pleasure to participating civil servants, is clear. Defining what for him is meant by 'A good job' he said: 'You need something which is of interest, you need something which is going to make a positive difference to the lives of others and the community or the environment. And you need to get that self-satisfaction from it' (Mr Farmer, HEO). Gaining pleasure and contentment from all of his activities, his well-being, and happiness are not simply a reflection of a balanced life, but of the value he places on the importance of its major aspects and being in the position of being able to achieve his goals in each.

Middle Grades: A Summary of Prominent Features

- Middle grade civil servants emphasise enjoyment of specific work tasks and appreciate having discrete responsibility for a certain role within their unit.
- Working structures which encouraged co-operative working arrangements are welcomed by this group. A number of features of work were identified which could damage co-operation, these were often aspects of work they found dissatisfying.
- Dissatisfactions at work included: staffing structures experienced as too many bosses; a high departmental workload; cuts and the damage to services; structural changes; problems with performance appraisal; insufficient promotion chances, and poor social relations with colleagues or supervisors.
- Many dislike change, some believe that experience is valued less than it once was.
- Positive aspects of their everyday lives identified by interviewees were able to help lessen the deleterious effects on mental health and

well-being of problems at work and outside. Mitigating features can include those aspects of work from which they gain satisfaction. Along with coping strategies, additional issues raised concern the particular context; valued work; social support, co-operation and collective action; leading a balanced life plus certain individual attitudes or personality factors such as taking a rational approach when encountering difficulties.

- Involvement in outside activities and through this achieving a work/life balance was an especially prominent feature of the group, perceived by respondents as beneficial to their mental health and well-being.
- Good mental health, well-being, and happiness are not simply a reflection of a balanced life, but of the value placed on the importance of its major aspects and being in the position to achieve desired goals in each.

CHAPTER 4

Higher Grades: 'You Have to Believe in the Value of What You Are Doing'

Abstract Expressions of the satisfaction gained from the work that they do were striking. Instrumental features include commitment and dedication to their work, their belief in its value, and contribution to the common good. Factors intervening between negative experience and mental health and well-being centred on material resources; the buffering or protective effects of a fulfilling work content; the meanings attached to the problem or to factors relating to it; protective coping strategies, which may reflect a strong sense of agency, and supportive colleagues. Satisfying work can act as a buffer to relationship, home, or work problems, an effect not restricted to the higher grades, but we could expect the greater the job satisfaction for an individual, the more effective the buffer. Work can be dissatisfying and frustrating when the imposition of work considered by the official to have little intrinsic value diverts their energies from what they perceived as valuable work. Whilst problems around control issues tend to be less dominant a feature of the work of higher grade civil servants a convergence of negative experiences can result in a perceived lack of control, while an over heavy workload could nullify the positive aspects of the job.

Keywords Satisfaction • Commitment • Value • Buffering • Coping • Workload • Agency • Social networks • Public service • Control

V. Cattell, S. Stansfeld, *Work in the Balance*,
https://doi.org/10.1007/978-3-031-96582-1_4

The higher grade group of civil servants include people who had begun their careers at a lower level, reaching posts at the lower rungs of the higher grades relatively late in their careers as well as people who entered at a level appropriate to degree level. The latter include some who were designated 'fast streamers', often from elite universities. There were a small number of examples of people on the lower end of the higher grade group (grade 7) whose experiences, attitudes, and values appeared to have had a little more in common with middle grades than with their higher grade colleagues. One grade 7, for example, got satisfaction from gaining recognition for what he does, from feeling appreciated, from people trusting him and asking his advice, or entrusting him with jobs to do, features also mentioned by colleagues in middle grades. Another exception to the general rule was a man less career-oriented than the majority of his colleagues. While a sense of status was important to him, this need was being met through his house and large garden, of which he was immensely proud, and not at his workplace; he acknowledged that he was not prepared to put in the time and effort necessary to achieve promotion, and, unusually for higher grades, never took work home.

Turning to the context of their working lives, as expected, higher grade civil servants overall enjoy a better standard of living than many of their middle grade or lower grade colleagues; financial difficulties were uncommon for example. They tend to live in attractive houses in desirable villages in the home counties or in leafy parts of London not too distant from their work and where population homogeneity—'fellow professionals'—was the norm. As well as contributing directly to their quality of life and a sense of well-being, the many material resources and advantages available to them also help higher grade civil servants to cope with home or work problems. Moving to an area which they chose fairly early in their careers, and were happy to continue living in, brought social advantages in terms of the community life which we associate with long-term residence and stable and supportive social networks.

Gaining Satisfaction from Work

Most higher grade civil servants gain a great deal of satisfaction from the work that they do. Motivated by a public service ethic for example, they derive pleasure from knowing they can make a difference to people's lives. Interviewees gave prominence to a wide range of factors including interesting and varied work; overcoming challenging tasks; commitment to and enjoyment of the subject matter of their remit along with the opportunity to build up expertise; good staff relations; a managerial role; policy work; decision-making and control; pride in the value of the work, and an adherence to a public service ethic as reasons for enjoying their work. An aspect viewed particularly positively is that they can exercise considerable choice, not only in the sense that they can decide what to prioritise, but that they are able to pick up on matters of especial interest to them or enjoy doing. Most individuals gained satisfaction from a wide number of the features mentioned, some of which did not stand alone but were recognised as needing to co-exist alongside others to be especially effective. Some respondents for example referred to the degree of control they exercised over the content of their job as significant for gaining job satisfaction from work variety. Officials who enjoyed dealing with particularly challenging endeavours mentioned issues such as 'turning round a job which had been a total mess', or 'teasing out problems'. A grade 2, Mr Judd, spoke of the rewards to be gained in overcoming a particular challenging task: 'Before giving a speaking engagement, I am in a paroxysm of nerves. But I do get a huge adrenalin rush from doing a big set piece occasion well; I get enormous personal satisfaction'. These officials included some who identified additional factors as necessary to be in place for a challenging job to be both enjoyable and beneficial to well-being, such as: 'work that stretches you without overload' or 'an equilibrium between work that is challenging, new and interesting, and reducing the pressure a bit'.

Creativity

The grade group covers a diversity of jobs; those in the professional/creative/scientific stratum, such as statisticians, scientists, designers, architects, and conservation experts, are both committed to and gain satisfaction from the professional content of the job. Their satisfaction and fulfilment result from the extent to which they are able to pursue their particular interests. As a statistician put it: 'If I can relate a problem to a mathematical formulation, then I am happy'. In another case, Mr Emin (7), a scientist, reported that although day to day work doesn't leave him enough time to do all the creative things he wants to do, he nevertheless gains much satisfaction from professional extracurricular activities, including writing for publication, and from the recognition he achieves from them. He explained: 'Sometimes you know, your best work is something you have done on the side. ... A lecture or a publication is gratifying because you get well, the equivalence of applause. … And you have got the evidence of your work in a publication. … I have always wanted the knowledge thing. … Having learned something new every day. … Finding patterns in the unknown—that really pleases me'.

Content of the Job

Many derive much enjoyment from the subject matter of their work. It was clear from interviews that officials, as well as being very committed to their remit, had built up a great deal of knowledge and expertise on their subject, something they found very satisfying indeed. Mrs Irving (5) for example described the pleasure she gained from becoming an expert in her field: 'I liked being Queen of my own patch', alongside additional elements of her role which she found satisfying: 'I liked having wider contacts made from international travel. I got lots of satisfaction from work and would like to have gone on enjoying it if I had not been pushed into something more restricting with restructuring'.

Whilst some amongst the grade group as a whole are not enthusiastic about taking on a largely managerial role, or, like some middle grades, made negative comments on departmental changes towards a managerialist culture involving, for example, target setting or the use of consultants, others reported that they gain satisfaction from working in a department that is well managed, and refer to their own role in the process. Specific aspects included: 'being able to build up a team'; 'getting agreement between parties'; 'being an instigator of change' and ensuring that a department's strong sense of purpose is inculcated to new staff. One referred to 'a managerial culture involving efficiency, a strong lead from the Permanent Secretary, systemising standards, values and ways of behaving, and tackling "gradism"' in this context (Mr Judd, 2).

In contrast many refer to the *policy* aspects of their work as a major source of pleasure, particular aspects of which, as for one grade 5 for example, involved 'Boiling down complex issues and progressing them co-operatively', or for another: 'Presenting policy to ministers and to the Permanent Secretary; you have influence over public affairs'. Some changes to the content of their job were welcomed, while others were not. Fast streamers described a Civil Service career as a much more demanding one than it used to be: 'When I joined you could thrive on a good brain and the ability to write well' (Mr Judd, 2); 'The Civil Service selects the fast stream to contribute to policy, but as you rose in your career you expected to manage staff and move away from these skills' (Mr Davis 3). Changes and new duties associated with promotion took Mr Davis's attention away from policy work, which he loved, and he felt ill at ease with and unsuited to his new management responsibilities as head of a division: 'I never was a prefect at school, while setting targets and budgets and not being able to continue with the intellectual side of a job was a problem for me'. The experience he believed had contributed to his subsequent depression.

Those who found both the policy and management aspects of their job enjoyable, included a man who relished the experience of playing several roles at once. An ideal job and real day to day satisfaction in what he was doing was for Mr Jameson (3) less about particular aspects of the content of the job, but: 'from being in alignment with your goals. And making progress to achieving those goals'.

Social Relations

Peers appeared, on the surface, to get on well, and most higher grade individuals spoke warmly of the staff reporting to them, citing team working, a democratic ethos, and camaraderie in this respect. For example: 'Your staff are your biggest asset. You look after them, and they will look after you' (Mr Urwin, 6); 'Once you've got a good team around you it could be immensely strong and there was a very nice democratic ethos' (Mrs Lawson, 7), which for Mrs Lawson meant a lack of grade consciousness. Similarly, Mr Judd (2) spoke positively about his own department's efforts in tackling gradism, which he defined as 'making assumptions that a lower grade person has an opinion which is less valuable'. Nonetheless, the situation could be interpreted differently by other grades, or by people in other ministries. A middle grade woman in one of the more traditional ministries described the frustration she felt when young, inexperienced higher grade fast streamers were given a free reign and power over staff in lower grades.

For some of the grade 5 women, enjoyment of the 'office community', and office camaraderie, were aspects of life which they had always considered important, and a reflection of the kind of togetherness experienced with other young people like themselves recruited into the Civil Service at the same time, or seconded to Brussels where there were opportunities to broaden contacts. Loyalty to one's colleagues was viewed as a product of good staff relations; one grade 5 expressed the belief that loyalty contributed to her department's good sickness record.

Pride in the Value of the Work Undertaken and a Public Service Ethic

Comments made when discussing enjoyable and valued aspects of work such as: 'I do actually think that what I am doing is an intrinsically important issue', were widespread amongst higher grades. In one example, a civil servant particularly enjoyed his work at a time when he was able to take pride in the *product* of what he was doing, in its quality: 'when we were world leaders … [in a particular type of public building]' (Mr Urwin, 6). All higher grade individuals taking part in this study stress the importance of the public service ethic to them. Ms Groom's (6) enjoyment of working on tasks such as a government bill is not unconnected to the satisfaction she gains from feeling that her work is improving the lot of the public, and can influence events. Mrs Enright (6) greatly values and gains personal self-esteem from work 'where you can see positive effects on the public of what you are doing'.

Meaningful Job Satisfaction

Overall, rather than focus on just one aspect of working life, officials interviewed across the higher grade range emphasise that several ingredients need to be in place at the same time for them to find meaningful satisfaction in their work. Examples include:

> 'stimulating colleagues; general enthusiasm in the air; the correct amount of work to do; some pressure, not too much pressure; recognition of your achievement, and learning new things'. (Mr Emin, 7)
>
> 'The subject matter; good colleagues; decent accommodation; being valued and getting positive feedback in the performance review'. (Mrs Lawson, 7)
>
> 'Work that stretches you without overload; good staff to share the load; a good boss who delegates and supports. When all the cogs in the wheel are there, it's an enjoyable place to be'. (Mrs Irving, 5)
>
> 'A degree of personal freedom to initiate, the ability to control your working day, a belief that what you are doing is of some worth, a constructive and stimulating set of colleagues, all are necessary conditions!'. (Mr Judd, 2)

Sources of Dissatisfaction

Most higher grades interviewed were not critical of the nature of the work itself, finding it highly interesting and believing it to be of value. Amongst problems raised were those related to: career paths; changes in the direction of managerialism; grade marking and performance related pay; organisational structures and re-organisation; difficulties with senior management; work pressure and overload, control issues and coinciding stressors.

Careers

Most of this group (the men especially) did not identify career progression as a serious problem or source of stress, describing the system as more open compared to the past when it was more difficult for middle grades to progress to higher for instance. Some remnants of the old system of preferential treatment given to fast streamers appeared to have persisted however: 'It is more flexible now, but the Civil Service still put more effort into looking after the careers of fast streamers than they do of other staff (Ms Groom, 6). Another in the group saw this kind of iniquity—'this residual attitude about their so-called superior abilities'—as the only downside to an otherwise enjoyable job (Mr Jameson, 3).

Whilst acknowledging that real steps had been taken to improve the situation, women were more critical of their experience of promotion opportunities than most of the men. Several identified a glass ceiling to their careers. A 'Paula Principle' (Schuller, 2017), that is, a tendency for women, but not men, to achieve posts below their level of competence, was manifested for some in perceptions of an effort/reward imbalance. Ms Stuart (5) reported that a huge amount of work was expected of her, but she was left with little prospect of further promotion. Structural inequalities associated with gender could even be seen to trump a fast streamer/ non fast streamer divide. Mrs Irving (5), added that, even for fast streamers, the careers of part timers, who were overwhelmingly female, were taken less seriously than those of full-time members of staff. Several women described their departmental culture as anti-women and male dominated and therefore indirectly discriminatory as well. In Mrs Copeman's (5) case, a male, macho, confrontational style of working was valued more, she believed, than her own consensus seeking management style involving co-operative forms of working such as getting people together to discuss issues and organising conferences. Her experiences have left her resentful of the way her career has progressed.

Grade Marking, Annual Reporting, and Performance Related Pay

Grade marking, mandatory annual reporting, and performance-related pay were viewed by higher grades as problems across all grades, if not necessarily for them. Nonetheless, carrying out staff appraisals was looked on as a negative or meaningless exercise as well as a beneficial one. Mrs Yeates (7) for example, found that writing annual reports—involving assessing performance against targets—became an increasingly labour-intensive exercise, something on a disproportionate scale which added to the weight of the job and produced material of doubtful value. Tellingly, she hated having to instruct staff to do things which she believed were 'a waste of time'.

Social Relations: Issues in Relation to Senior Management

Difficulties concerning social relations amongst peers were rarely mentioned, but problems with senior management occasionally were. Examples included Mrs Lawson's (7) experience of a manager ducking responsibility to the detriment of the well-being of his staff by not informing them that their work was being abandoned and their jobs no longer secure, and an account of another manager's actions which led to individuals reporting to them experiencing an effort/reward imbalance. As Mrs Lawson (7) described it: 'When you get a negative reaction to a piece of work when you were expecting a positive one, and you'd invested a great deal of time and energy in it, then that is stressful'. A separate case concerns Mrs Yeates, another grade 7 woman who was understandably furious when 'in a year when I put on a major exhibition and wrote 3 publications, I did not get the top grade on my annual report'. She made a formal complaint and found it a very stressful time. The same official spoke about the long-term effects of a particularly stressful experience. Her boss humiliated her in a formal meeting of about 30 people: 'and he just put me down in front of all those people, in a really bad way, and I remember I just sat there and swallowed my humiliation. You know moments like that you never forget, and I'll never forgive him for it. I wonder if he felt ashamed when he saw what I was working on and what I'd done'. She recalls that she must have been on the verge of a nervous breakdown at the time. A male grade 2 acknowledged that problems like this existed: 'Peers treat each other with respect, but some senior people do not treat their staff with enough respect, a reflection of Ministers taking us for granted too'.

Pressure, Overload, and Insufficient Control

Almost all of those interviewed in this group identified a high volume of work as a source of stress, often alongside perceptions of diminishing control. Examples included: having to do things at a faster pace than feeling happy with; having to meet deadlines yet wanting to meet one's own expectations on quality; getting through more than feeling capable of doing and having to take work home in order to meet their various responsibilities; and needing to cut corners to keep up with the pressure and high volume of work. Respondents mentioned some of the repercussions of an overload of work. For example:

- Overburdened managers were left with less time to talk to their staff: 'It was very stressful when you needed to discuss a matter with someone, and they were never available'.
- Conflicting demands could exacerbate the negative effects of too high a workload: 'They were telling us to spend more time … talking and listening to staff, but at the same time they were throwing more and more work at us. It wasn't capable of resolution'.
- The removal of one of the intermediate rungs between grade 2 and grade 5, meant that strategic direction or support for grade fives in dealing with Ministers could be negatively affected. At the same time, work overload and the obligation to take it on, together with a lack of staffing to delegate to or of supportive direction from senior management, left a grade 5, for example, feeling especially out of control.

A long hours departmental culture with a focus on fast decisions and quick results, described as 'anti-theoretical', could also exacerbate overload related pressure. Higher grades appeared to face a choice in these contexts between struggling with an over heavy workload and experiencing stress on the one hand, or, retiring early to avoid these problems but leaving a job which had been intrinsically interesting and satisfying and from which they gained respect and self-esteem.

Generally, control issues tend to be less dominant a feature of the work of higher grade individuals compared to lower grade colleagues; the study confirmed that the degree of decision latitude was grade related. Nevertheless, some identified circumstances additional to those already mentioned under which they felt less in control than they wished. Changes in the structure of decision-making were mentioned for example, as were internal politics covering issues such as competitive roles in relations with other groups.

An increasing workload, or a reduction in decision latitude were both seen as driving a stressful work experience. Mrs Copeman (7) for example described the effects on her department of cuts in resources: 'We are not in control ... we haven't got enough staff and we haven't got the staff of the right calibre to do the work'. Referring to colleagues who had experienced depression related to a heavy burden of work she added that: 'Civil servants are often very conscientious; when high demands are made on them, they go under'. An overload of work combined with low control/ decision latitude were confirmed as especially stressful. Ms Stuart (5), for example feels out of control when her workload is unpredictable and when at the same time, she is reliant on others as her job involves co-ordination with colleagues. Comparing her last post unfavourably with her present one she explained: 'The main pressure was the unpredictability of my working hours. In my last job I really had so much to do, and there were times when I just didn't seem to do anything but get up, eat, go to work, come home, eat, and go to bed. And I was really annoyed then because I don't like just spending all my life working and I felt pretty out of control. And because my job involved a good deal of co-ordination, I was reliant on other people a lot, so I had no idea when I was going to be working long hours'. Describing the effects on her free time she added: 'Outside of work I'm quite organised, so I have a reasonable measure of control. The problem is when you're trying to fit a lot in, you do risk becoming a control freak; somebody rings you up and you think "God I'm only scheduled 10 minutes with this telephone call, get off", which is silly. ... On the other hand if you're single and live alone you can't just sit around and wait for life to happen, so you have to have some organisation' (Ms Stuart, 5).

Critically, the damaging effects of experiencing high demands plus low control on mental health and well-being can be exacerbated when certain *meanings* of work, and in particular the value individuals assign to particular bodies of work, are taken into account. While, as Ms Groom (6) explains, she resents occasions when she has to do things at a pace she considers is too fast, or prioritise something because of where it has come from rather than make the decision herself, it is having to give priority to something which she considers trivial which makes her feel especially distressed and out of control. Similarly, for Mrs Whiting (5), Departmental initiatives which she considered to have little intrinsic value, were diverting her energies from her own remit, from what she perceived as valuable work.

Multiple Stressors

Higher grades were generally better resourced and experienced fewer stressors than individuals in other grades, but that is not to say they did not have experiences which could precipitate mental illness. Where a coincidence of stressors was apparent—involving multiple problems at work or difficulties at both work and home or in other aspects of one's life—and when supports were temporarily weakened, then even a favourably positioned individual could be at risk. Mr Urwin's (6) case highlighted the effects of a combination of stressors at work. In his case they involved: 'A disastrous computer project'; having 'some dud staff dumped' on him; the threat of re-organisation, and a planned departmental move to another city. 'You could have coped with one of these, but not all four at once. I experienced 6 years of huge stress'. Yet, he added, before this, he had never done anything at work which he did not enjoy.

A grade 3 man, who lived in a very pleasant part of outer London, enjoyed a good income and was integrated into local activities via his wife, nevertheless went through a time when he experienced stress in most aspects of his life: 'I felt out of control. In my own experience feeling in control involves a proper balance between work and home and a reasonably good environment in both, and supportive in both. At times it hasn't been either. I had too many things…going on'. His children were taking exams, a parent died, and at the same time he was promoted at work. His new duties left less time for the policy work which he loved, and he felt ill at ease with and unsuited to his increased management responsibilities. These, together with more generalised stressors, such as a deterioration in working relationships between officials and ministers at the time, precipitated a serious depression. He would normally rely on his wife for support, but she was taking on more voluntary work at the time, and he felt that she had little understanding of his state of mind and need for help. When referring to the death of one of his parents, he explained a predilection on his part to be over conscientious by referring to his relationship with his parents and acknowledged a tendency of struggling to earn their esteem throughout his life.

Mrs Irving (5) found that the volume of work together with extra family demands became unmanageable when new departmental initiatives were suddenly introduced. When several sources of stress coincide to the detriment of well-being, a heavy workload is frequently a key component. A male grade 2 recognises that an intense work schedule together with time spent travelling from his house in the Home Counties to offices in both London and a city in the North of England, damages his health. He suffers regularly from bouts of anxiety and depression. Putting his episodes of mental ill health and treatment with anti-depressants into context he said: 'It is associated with times of high pressure at work, but when it is combined with high pressure at home then it becomes particularly marked. At work, two departments merged, and I found my new post demanding. At the same time, I felt particularly out of control at home, my wife and I had different priorities over our work commitments and could not work it out together'. When additional home or work problems arise which, under more normal circumstances would not be seen as problems perhaps, they can trigger effects even more acute than those already experienced. Speaking of a temporarily overcrowded home environment he added: 'It really gets to me'.

Intermediate Factors Protecting Well-Being, Minimising, Or Driving Stress

Factors indicated by higher grades as intervening between negative experience and mental health and well-being were many. They centred on material resources; the buffering or protective effects of a fulfilling work content; the meanings attached to the problem or to factors relating to it; protective coping strategies—which may reflect a strong sense of agency; supportive and co-operative colleagues, and the ability or opportunity to lead a balanced life.

Resources and Advantages Alleviating Potential Stressors

As well as contributing directly to their quality of life and sense of well-being, the many resources and advantages available to them and the choices they provide help higher grade civil servants to cope with home or work problems: spending money to get a relative out of difficulties; buying a flat for a son or daughter with problems; using their equally well-resourced social networks to gain information or help solve work-related problems, or exiting a stressful work situation by taking early retirement backed by the security of an adequate pension income or inherited wealth. As a grade 7 said when referring to a parent who needed help: 'I'm not too worried about spending money to solve problems'. For some respondents, a second home in attractive surroundings, with good facilities and opportunities for enjoyable leisure pursuits, was not only of direct benefit to their quality of life, by providing a base from which to better organise one's social life for example, but also reduced the potential stress effect of work overload problems by lessoning the burden or nuisance value of taking work home at weekends and gaining pleasure from working in beautiful surroundings.

High Satisfaction from the Content of Work

One of the most salient and advantageous factors found to mediate between negative experience and mental health and well-being centred on work as a pleasurable experience. Along with several other higher grades, work difficulties or changes for Mr Taylor (7) for example, were offset by the very high levels of satisfaction gained from the content of the work itself. Like many of the professionals in the study, Mr Williams (7) is very happy in the job he is doing, and, because of this, career progression in his case assumes less importance for him: 'I might get lucky and move one level up, but would not want it if I did not enjoy what I was doing'. Several of the professional officials reported that as long as they were able to pursue their particular interests—creative work which had positive meaning for them—potentially damaging experiences such as limited promotion opportunities, difficult relations with a section head, problems with 'red tape', or the introduction of new and unpopular initiatives, generally left them unscathed. They felt able to distance themselves from these difficulties. Additionally, and for the grade as a whole, satisfying work can act as a buffer to relationship or home problems, an effect not restricted to the higher grades, but clearly we could expect the greater the job satisfaction for an individual, the more effective the buffer.

Coping Strategies

As well as the advantages associated with material resources and enjoyment of their work, higher grade civil servants also discussed their active coping strategies for addressing particular problems at work. These include taking work home; managing and using contacts; prioritising tasks; taking tea breaks; talking therapy; avoidance; taking pains to right a wrong; and displaying a strong sense of agency in general.

Taking work home for example is a common coping strategy for this grade group for whom increasing workloads and the expectations and obligations associated with a long hours culture can be a source of stress. As one said: ‘working longer … makes home life much reduced and much less fun’ (Mrs Copeman, 5). Thus coping in one major strand of one’s life is achieved but at the expense of another.

Cognitive Behavioural Therapy

Like some of those in lower and middle grade groups, higher grade civil servants sought out talking therapies and found them helpful for getting them through a crisis. During a period of simultaneously arising difficulties, Mr Davis (3) reported that he had no one to go to for emotional support: ‘It all tended to get bottled up. Of course, some would have gone off and had an affair or taken to drink, but I didn’t do either of these. But now, as a result of the cognitive therapy I try to avoid things that cause me anxiety [such as taking on legal problems for relatives outside his immediate family]. … I’ve always been a willing horse … but I can say no now’.

Collective Support

Some respondents sought support collectively at work. Mrs Irving (5) for example, was part of an informal support group of part timers who took their problems to management together. In another example, Mrs Meade, 7, who described her personal appraisal reports as ‘a joke’, refused to sign hers; she and her colleagues took out a collective grievance procedure which resulted in positive changes the following year. Mr Urwin (6) found a different form of mutual support to be helpful when tackling certain issues. He described a time when his department was undergoing difficult changes as one of 'strong camaraderie and respect between people. We didn't find solutions, but just talking things over helped'. The benefits of talking to colleagues may not be restricted to situations where discussions centre on a particular shared problem, but can also help civil servants to temporarily escape from difficulties as well. Mr Emin (7) acknowledges that he is very sensitive to criticism, and tends to brood. To avoid a work-based source of stress, in his case an overly critical colleague with whom he shares an office, he takes regular tea breaks with like-minded professional colleagues.

Rationality, Agency, and Confidence

We gained a sense from interviews that many of these men and women put much effort into coping: some believed that their efforts were able to protect them from the effects of stressful experiences. Mrs Irving (5) for example acknowledged that: 'I've had a pretty satisfactory life, but I feel that I've put quite a lot into it myself'. Some of these higher grades were fast streamers, confident that they could succeed. Not all fell into this category. Coming from a 'family of copers', Mr Urwin's (6) ability to cope he reported, stemmed from his early experiences. He was brought up to face problems and overcome them. To deal with several very stressful changes necessitating taking work home every night and at weekends, he emphasised that: 'I always cope however, I did not break down. Whatever happens you just get on with it'. Mr Emsley, who began his career on a much lower grade and yet had attained a grade 5 position, emphasised that, because he experienced conflicting demands constantly, then prioritising them was essential. Mrs Enright (6) is also amongst civil servants who take a rational approach to work and home problems by prioritising and negotiating. She finds caring for her sick father stressful, and something which impacts on her work, her leisure time, and her happiness. To cope, she 'spends every minute' thinking about how she can organise situations: 'I have had to do a fair bit of work at home, and rely more on my staff. They are a good bunch and will co-operate to remedy a problem'. Ms Stuart (5) turns problems and challenges into pleasurable activity, she enjoys working out work difficulties along with her staff: 'I like seeing how we can manage things better'. A serious problem occurred for Mrs Copeman (5) when she was accused (wrongly) in the press of scuppering an initiative, even receiving hate mail. The problem lay in the politicisation of her role, yet, as a public servant, she could not defend herself publicly. Instead she coped actively with the situation directly herself, by writing individually to everyone who had contacted her to explain what she had done and why.

Wide Networks and Managing Contacts

Quite a strong feature of civil servants in this grade group concerned the effort they put into managing a wide circle of contacts effectively. Mrs Yeates (7) for example, has gained friends from work, from university, and from involvement in local activities, as well as from contacts made when working abroad, friendship networks which were able to compensate for a lack of support from relatives when experiencing stressful situations at home. Mrs Copeman (5) also has wide ties, both dense and loose, her siblings are very supportive to each other, and she has many friends in both London and in the place where she has a weekend home. Some of her loose ties provide very direct benefits. She is a member of the committee of her old Oxbridge College, for example, a useful resource providing access to a directory of contacts which she uses to find people with background knowledge to help her with aspects of her work. Similarly, Mrs Meade (7) used her loose ties to help her perform her job effectively and cope with a difficult and disaffecting period at work when the workload increased and her department was downsized. These were conditions she believed which made it more difficult to arrive at good policy. 'Good policy costs money', she insisted, and being able to achieve the right policy was very important to her. Her response was to actively manage the situation through using the many contacts made in her professional work before joining the Civil Service to help inform the direction of policy. She sought advice, carried out consultation exercises, and held conferences. In these different cases, higher grade individuals' access to well-informed and resourced social networks helps them to perform their work effectively, an aspect of life which they value highly.

The strong sense of agency already noted, and along with it the development of self-confidence, are reflected also in ways in which higher grades maintain supportive personal contacts made outside work. Despite an extremely heavy workload which makes any kind of outside life almost impossible, a grade 2 nonetheless manages to keep in touch with a close, supportive, and valued group of friends from boarding school. Recently retired respondents were better placed than some working colleagues to develop and sustain current contacts. Mrs Lawson (7) for example, is very active in local societies and actively manages her wide social networks. Consequently, whenever she needs help, information, or advice, there is always someone appropriate to contact. Similarly, Mrs Irving (5), puts considerable effort into organising her social networks and social life effectively, insisting: 'It's a policy on my part to try and do that'. A benefit for her is feeling in control of her life.

Achieving a Balance Between Work and Life Outside

Like middle grade colleagues, certain higher grade civil servants, especially those at the slightly lower end of this grade group, were enjoying a balanced life in the sense of gaining satisfaction from aspects of both work and life outside, in having a rich voluntary life or being able to pursue interests which could mitigate work pressures as well as being of direct benefit. Ms Groom (6) for example, speaking of personal relationships, said: 'work can be a crutch to keep them going, and relationships are important for people to function at work'. Ms Stuart (5) reported that she copes with stress at work by getting involved in local activities, and thereby ensuring that work is not her whole life. She believes that: 'you can tot up a positive balance if there are positive aspects to your life'. Involvement in social or musical activities contributed towards a general sense of enjoyment and well-being for Mr Emin (7). Having a good time at rehearsals, and the enjoyable get-togethers in the pub afterwards, had a mediating as well as a more direct effect on his well-being. These activities cheered him up when he was experiencing work difficulties and feeling low, as well as facilitating emotional support from the others involved: 'People keep you going. It's a treat to mix with singing friends, I feel so much better afterwards … mixing with positive people is a boost'.

For some fortunate individuals, a balanced life takes a broad form. Mr Emsley (5) describes his home as: 'a very nice house in a very nice area' and mentions friendly and supportive neighbours. He plays in a band as a hobby, something which he finds a very positive experience. The activity is not without its pressures, but he explained: 'it's a *different kind of pressure* from work pressure', and acts as a distraction perhaps. He also appreciates having the very mixed networks his pastimes facilitate. Mr Williams's (7) balanced life seemingly encompasses most aspects of his life. He enjoys and derives pleasure from his work as a specialist scientist, from his home and neighbourhood, his leisure activities, and his marriage. He describes his house and the surrounding countryside as lovely yet within an easy commuting distance, and he regularly socialises, holidays, and co-operates with his neighbours, some of whom have become firm friends. He reported that he is a happy person; potentially negative experiences seem to have done little to dent his esteem, confidence, and contentment.

Additional reasons for why these officials find a balanced life beneficial include those centred on the meanings that their activities have for them. Heavily involved in local voluntary pursuits, Ms Stuart (5), mentioned above, explained that she derived happiness from a feeling of belonging, from being integrated into a community both at home and at work. She is highly committed to the part of London where she lives; for her, a good neighbourhood meant: 'commitment, and a sense of common values and standards'. She explained her attitudes in terms of experiencing a close community when a child, and links her strong volunteering ethos together with a strong sense of injustice to the influence of her politically active family.

We could reasonably expect that a balanced life would increase the likelihood that individuals' foremost needs are met. For Mr Emin (7) for example, work and musical activities both satisfy his need for creativity and recognition. In Mr Williams's, (7) case, a good job means gaining satisfaction from co-operating with colleagues and trusting your head of division, as well as from doing what you want to do and from not being side-lined. All of which he has. Getting on with people in life generally is also important for him, for example: 'I don't like confrontation ... to live in conflict with your neighbours would be unbearable, I think it would make me very stressed'.

A work/life balance appeared to be more difficult to achieve for higher grades in the more senior positions. For Mr Judd (2), an overload of work, together with a working week involving an onerous three way commute (he describes himself as having 'no fixed abode') are damaging to any kind of meaningful equilibrium. Time constraints are curtailing interaction with his wife, family, friends, and local community. He has had to give up the local involvement which he used to enjoy for example. Additionally, practical issues like house maintenance problems go un-dealt with making life at home more difficult. He suffers regularly from bouts of anxiety and depression and, because he recognises the effects of his intense work schedule on the satisfaction he once attained from his job, was intending to retire earlier than he had originally planned. The example illustrates circumstances in which the burden of an excessive workload appears to cut across and negate the many positive aspects of an individual's life and work.

Orientations: The Strength of Meanings Related to Work

Higher grades' orientations to work, that is, factors which hold significantly profound meanings for them, include expectations of career progression, adherence to a public service ethic, and a high level of commitment to their work.

Expectation of Progressing Careers/Status Orientation

When considering higher grades' expectations of advancing careers, it can be helpful to look at the lives of fast streamers, not simply as a meritocracy, but as a continuum, a constant over working lives. There was an underlying optimism apparent here, an expectation that life would always be good, and that careers would continue to progress. A long-held optimism perhaps is something which can distinguish them from many in other groups. Having confidence, both in themselves and in the future, appeared linked with motivational behaviour: they expect the effort they put into their endeavours to pay dividends. Bridging social capital which involves a wide spectrum of diverse social contacts seems, as here, to provide richly supportive resources. Bridging social capital has been shown to have a stronger effect on mental health than bonding social capital (Pedersen et al., 2023).

When careers, albeit found in relatively rare cases, are abruptly truncated however, the experience can be especially distressing for the individual concerned. For Mrs Irving (5) re-organisation entailed a drop in status for her part-time post as well as less interesting work: 'So having been equal to other people at the same grade you suddenly were quite clearly viewed as right down there'. She found the experience demoralising and stressful and responded by accepting an offer of early retirement.

An Ethic of Public Service

A strong subscription to a public service ethic was apparent in all higher grade civil servants interviewed for this study. For Mr Urwin (6), an ideal job for example, involves: 'contributing to the well-being of the nation'. Some gain a personal sense of self-esteem from their adherence to public service. For Mrs Enright (6) for example, a public service ethic involves: 'Seeing positive effects on the public of what you are doing, or developing a policy that is going to make a difference. ... Then you can respect yourself at the end of the day'. A grade three official, Mr Jameson, who had recently moved into the private sector from the Civil Service, found his new job less taxing, but nevertheless demoralising because he saw little value in it: 'and that's stressful if you don't really believe in it'. In a similar manner, and within the Service, a stressful situation can occur when demands of loyalty to a public service ethic, of obedience, and Civil Service neutrality conflict. As one high grade man suggested, a committed official who then has to work with politicians whose policies he or she believes are not contributing to the common good, could be expected to experience some ensuing strain.

Mrs Copeman (5) like many others in this group, is committed to working on policy which will improve people's lives, attitudes in her case influenced to some extent by her father, who was also a public servant. As already mentioned, when working on a commission she was wrongly accused by the press and a pressure group of scuppering an initiative, and even received hate mail. The meaning that the work held for her made the accusations more wounding however. Not only had she worked really hard to get it right, but she also perceived the work to be highly important. She described the episode as a searing experience, and one which left her feeling distrustful, angry, and 'quite depressed' for a while. An element of effort/reward imbalance combined with a certain amount of diminishing control may have been evident here, but the central issue for her was the unfair reaction on the part of others to a piece of work of which she not only felt proud but which she believed had the potential to be highly beneficial to the public at large.

Motivating values involving the commitment and dedication to their work and a belief in its contribution to the common good were also sustained in the lives of men and women who had recently retired when interviewed and who then directed their energies towards the voluntary sector, some taking up posts at a senior level. For example, a grade 5 woman gains satisfaction from 'doing something for the community' by sharing her skills and interests, while a grade 6 man finds involvement rewarding and values the opportunity to 'put something back'. In contrast to these examples, individuals interviewed at the upper end of the higher grade spectrum who were still working were not participating in local or national organisations—their workload does not facilitate it—but were planning to find some space to be active citizens on retirement, seeing a continuing role for themselves in trying to improve things.

Commitment to Work

Commitment to a public service ethic and commitment to the policy area they work in are frequently inter-linked in respondents' thoughts on these subjects. Mr Urwin (6) had been immensely proud of the quality of the work his unit once produced, and was gratified that it was seen as successful and valued by others worldwide. But, he reported: 'Politicians destroyed it all for political reasons'. The experience of re-organisation he found especially distressing as the quality of the end result was compromised. He insisted that: 'You have to believe in the value of what you are doing'.

While almost all of the higher grade staff taking part in the study were highly committed to their work overall, some placed particular emphasis on certain features. They may be especially enthusiastic about policy work, or management, about their remit or pursuance of a creative role. The creative side of Mr Emin's (7) work, for example, is so essential to him that that he looks forward to continuing to do what he enjoys and gains recognition for when he retires. For Mrs Yeates (7) a woman for whom: 'Work has been the most important thing in my life', creativity is pivotal. Referring to an unsupportive boss she said: 'Anxiety about whether one can achieve is part of the creative process, it is what wakes you at night. It's made worse however when people are obstructing you'. She added 'Committed creative people must be given freedom to do what they want to do and be given the support they need'.

In all cases, where additional and unwelcome demands, structural changes, or even promotion take them away from or impede what they perceive as valuable work, the result can be frustration or anxiety. Some reported feeling out of control in situations where the demands made were external for example, where certain work had to be prioritised because of a governmental or departmental diktat. For Mrs Whiting (5), the new initiatives one was expected to do in her department were a hindrance to what to her, was the more important work: 'I'd be negotiating on two important directives, at a crucial stage of negotiations, when suddenly you'd be asked to do some ridiculous exercise which would have to be completed in 24 hours'. Again, an ensuing demand/control imbalance can be recognised here, but consideration of meanings highlights more nuanced issues. The demands—'some ridiculous exercise'—were believed by Mrs Yeates as having little merit when compared to her ongoing, regular work, which she perceived as highly valuable.

The Downside of Commitment

The high degree of commitment to their work displayed by the majority here can for some, be a two edged sword. Dedication may need to be of a strength such that extraneous aspects of life are neglected or overridden. While the needs of the organisation are being met, the needs of individuals, such as those for a work/life balance, may be relegated in importance. Mr Judd (2) for example acknowledges the value he places on the puritan work ethic and on his particular remit at work: 'I think that what I am doing here is an extremely important issue'. He prioritises work problems including an excessive workload over home problems so that his work does not suffer, but *he* clearly does. A situation which developed leaving him little time to spend with his family and with only tenuous links with the local community he once enjoyed being a part of, acted as a strong contributor to his periods of anxiety and depression.

Mr Judd's (2) case suggests some important points for our understanding of work characteristics and mental ill health. His work-related needs, that is, for 'a degree of personal freedom to initiate, the ability to control your working day, a belief that what you are doing is of some worth, and a constructive and stimulating set of colleagues', as well as enjoyment derived from 'writing, talking and teasing out problems', were all being met. Yet despite having the kind of job which is important to him, an over heavy workload and resulting burnout can be seen as negating them all. He added that 'I suppose if I am absolutely honest, I get less satisfaction out of it now than I used to. I get increasingly frustrated with some of the downsides of the job'. Given the volume of work, he did not feel entirely in control of it.

A work-life balance was identified as beneficial to mental health and well-being among a number of staff in the study, across grades. Those for whom most aspects of work and life outside are important to them and enjoyable could be seen to be achieving a balance between what Durkheim (1952) referred to as egoism—in this context, personal satisfaction from activities at work and at home—and altruism, in the sense of adherence to a public service ethic involving a commitment to serving others. In contrast, in cases where a very high commitment to the work or to public service threatens work/life equilibrium, as it did for some of the more senior CS—it became apparent that excessive altruism was damaging their health and well-being.

Higher Grade Civil Servants: A Summary of Prominent Features

Features which stand out as typical of the working experience of higher grades include:

- Gaining a great deal of satisfaction from the work that they do. Most individuals derived enjoyment from a wide number of factors many of which did not stand alone but were recognised as needing to co-exist with others to achieve meaningful job satisfaction.
- An over heavy workload was a common experience. When several sources of stress coincide, to the detriment of well-being, a heavy workload is frequently a key component.
- Factors indicated by higher grades as intervening between negative experience and mental health and well-being were many and centred on material resources; the buffering or protective effects of a fulfilling work content; the meanings attached to the problem or to factors relating to it; protective coping strategies, which may reflect a strong sense of agency; supportive and co-operative colleagues, and the ability to lead a balanced life.
- Satisfying work can act as a buffer to relationship, home, or work problems, an effect not restricted to the higher grades, but we could expect the greater the job satisfaction for an individual, the more effective the buffer.
- A strong sense of agency was evident. These civil servants report that they put a great deal of effort into coping with problems and stressful experiences.
- Higher grade individuals' access to well-informed and resourced social networks (such as contacts made at elite universities) help

them to perform their work effectively, an aspect of life which they value highly.

- A balanced life was valued. Some overworked individuals were unable to achieve it.
- A high level of commitment and dedication to their work and their belief in its contribution to the common good stood out most clearly from these interviews. Work can be dissatisfying and frustrating when the imposition of work considered by the official to have little intrinsic value diverts their energies from what they perceived as valuable work.

References

Schuller, T. (2017). *The Paula Principle: How and Why Women Work Below Their Level of Competence*. Scribe.

Durkheim, E. (1952). *Suicide a study in sociology*. Routledge.

Pedersen, L. M., Laursen, S., & Buttenschøn, H. N. (2023). Is mental health positively associated with workplace social capital among Danish hospital employees? A multilevel study. *Mental Health & Prevention, 32*, 200–300.

CHAPTER 5

Conclusions: Richer Lives

Abstract Coping resources tend to increase with grade level. The meaning invested in both stressors/difficulties and resources/advantages for individuals play a significant role here in the severity of their impact or strength of their effectiveness. Considerations of meanings helps widen our understanding of the role of psychosocial pathways such as confidence, esteem, and perceptions of control in relationships between stressful experience and mental health and well-being. The findings in an earlier Whitehall II quantitative study which showed that social support does not explain the grade gradient in depression can be better understood with reference to grade variation in (a) the meaning and value of social relations and support; (b) the structure of social ties and their enabling access to resources; and (c) the additional resources and positive features of work and life outside available to individuals. This book notes the necessary reliance on social ties for lower grades, who have fewer additional resources at their disposal.

We have witnessed a growth nationally in work-related mental ill health since 2010, and an increase in poor quality work. This book emphasises that satisfying features of work are not evenly distributed across employment grades in the study.

Keywords Coping • Stress • Resources • Meanings • Psychosocial • Social capital • Social networks • Work • Quality • Inequalities

V. Cattell, S. Stansfeld, *Work in the Balance*,
https://doi.org/10.1007/978-3-031-96582-1_5

As well as illustrating some of the damaging effects of the working environment, previous chapters have highlighted the positive value of work to the well-being of the individual. Our findings demonstrate grade variation as well as commonality in the breadth and kinds of stressors experienced and resources available to people in their working lives and outside paid employment and consider some of the meanings invested in them. A source of satisfaction for example found in all three groups, but which substantially increased with level of seniority, concerned a belief in the value of the work undertaken. Another involved good or co-operative social relations, which in this case, was mentioned more frequently with decreasing grade. Common dissatisfactions and stressors across grades included work overload, workplace change, negative experience of the annual reporting system (triggering a sense of injustice), and a lack of promotion for those, especially amongst middle and lower grades, who desired or expected it. Higher grade women interviewed resented a perceived 'glass ceiling'. The especially deleterious effects of a combination of stressors occurring at one time were commonly experienced.

Prominent Features of Grade Groups

Despite a diversity of jobs in each, and occasionally fluid lines between group divisions, grade groups were readily distinguished by the prominence of certain features. Particular stressors deriving from the workplace can be more common in lower grades, a lack of confidence when performing new tasks without adequate training was experienced as stressful for example, as were difficult relationships, routine, communication problems, uncertainty about the future, dysfunctional work units, and feeling alienated from the working environment. Lower grades on the whole did not expect to gain much satisfaction from the actual content of the work, but potential difficulties like performing routine tasks, for example, were not necessarily a problem if they gained enjoyment from other aspects of the job. The most prominent feature of this grade group was the primacy of experiencing good social relations and positive, friendly, and supportive social ties at work and outside work, of being integrated into a cohesive, friendly, co-operative, and solidaristic work group or community. Mixing with colleagues, for example, was identified as an especially enjoyable aspect of their job. Positive social relationships could mitigate specific negatively perceived work characteristics as well as carry direct benefits; where good working relationships with peers and bosses were disrupted by re-organisation involving changes in the social organisation of the department or unit, the workplace could become a source of stress. In line with work by Malik et al. (2021), for example, who noted that interpersonal workplace conflict is one of the greatest contributors to stressful experience, we found poor social relations and conflict, especially with line managers and supervisors—and which occasionally could involve allegations of bullying—were a common cause of dissatisfaction and perceptions of injustice for lower grades. Overall, the need for and reliance on social support to help with difficulties was the foremost characteristic of this group. Rapid re-organisation may undermine relations between managers and lower grades with a loss of what Sennett (2013) calls 'earned authority', the respect that employers have for managers who fully engage with employees.

Middle grade civil servants by contrast were able to pinpoint their enjoyment of specific work tasks and mentioned job clarity, which included discrete responsibility for a certain role within their unit, in this context. Working structures which encourage teamwork and co-operative working arrangements are appreciated as is an understanding for some that their work is of value. Sennett (1998) has suggested that employees today are expected to be less reliant on regulations and formal procedures, but many of our middle grade civil servants dislike change, and some believe that experience is now appreciated less, that the certainty of career progression had gone, and that order and predictability were being eroded. New reporting systems were a general source of anxiety, not least because an effect could be to damage co-operation with peers, generally viewed as a positive feature of their work, as well as hamper their own promotion prospects. Involvement in outside activities and through this achieving a work-life balance was an especially prominent feature of the group, something valued highly by respondents and, confirming work by Putnam (2000), Kawachi et al. (2010) and others, understood by them as beneficial to their psychological health, and is a major contributor to job satisfaction (Findlay & Thompson, 2017).

Along with experiencing a good standard of living and its benefits in relation to coping with stressful issues, features which stand out as typical of the experience of higher grades include commitment and dedication to their work, their belief in its value and contribution to the common good, and that problems can be remedied. Higher grades tend to have a clear sense of purpose, and are goal focused. A powerful sense of agency is driven by strong feelings of confidence, by a belief that life will continue to improve and careers develop, that they can achieve success, and that problems can be remedied. A keen sense of agency on their part can impel individuals to take control of tricky situations. Expressions of the great deal of satisfaction gained from the work that they do were striking, something gained from a wide number of factors. Work was considered dissatisfying and frustrating however when control shifted, when the imposition of governmental directives or departmental initiatives considered by the official to have little intrinsic value needed to be given priority and divert energies from what they perceived as valuable work. An over heavy workload was a common experience, and one which, for certain individuals, could act to nullify the positive aspects of the job and have a detrimental impact on mental health and well-being.

Perceptions of Control

Pathways to good or poor mental health and well-being alluded to by people taking part in the study include perceptions of control, self-esteem, or contentment; gaining a sense of achievement; being shown appreciation; experiencing bitterness and a sense of injustice, and feelings of hope or hopelessness, as well as valuing and being committed to their work. The study confirms earlier work (Stansfeld et al., 1999; Stansfeld & Candy, 2006) demonstrating perceptions of control as especially important pathways in processes involved in mental health and well-being. A generally used definition of perceptions of control in the literature concerns the belief that 'one can determine one's own internal states and behaviour, influence one's environment, and/or bring about desired outcomes' (Wallston et al., 1987). At a basic level, some participants in this study consider feeling in control as life going well, living the life they want to lead, whether this concerns family, local involvement, or satisfactions gained in the workplace. Feeling in control can be corroded when these positive aspects of lives are compromised. For some individuals, a personal need for being in control was also apparent.

For lower grade civil servants taking part in the study, feeling out of control could be commonly expressed. Understandings of a lack of control (sometimes expressed as powerlessness) were associated with a number of factors including:

- Low financial resources and debt.

- Feeling overloaded with tasks and having to complete to a particular timescale.
- Having to cope with new and unfamiliar tasks without adequate training.
- Difficulties with new and unfamiliar locations.
- Uncertainty concerning redundancies and additional work issues, future living arrangements, or the outcome of a relative's illness.
- Perceptions of organisational injustice, of being treated unfairly, or criticised unfairly.
- Interference with work tasks.
- A co-incidence of stressors involving work, home, or health issues, which could leave those experiencing them with little energy to rectify a problem.
- Examples of particularly acute perceptions of powerlessness amongst lower grades were linked to:

  - An inability to settle a problem because help from senior management or the union was not available.
  - Alienation from the work tasks, the product of the work, and from colleagues.

Our analysis suggests that perceptions of lack of control can have increasing significance for people at various stages of the stress process, a pattern which has especial relevance to the experience of our lower grade group: (1) experiencing an objective or structured lack of control at work in a job closely supervised or responding to the needs and instructions of others; (2) experiencing problems and difficulties; (3) having insufficient coping resources or feeling options blocked; and (4) becoming anxious or depressed.

A two-way process was seen to occur when we considered relationships between stress and perceptions of control more closely. A lack of control was recounted by individuals as both a cause and product of stress. For example, feeling powerless within the structure of a particular work unit impacted on lower grade civil servants' ability to solve a work problem, whilst an inability to rectify the problematic situation re-enforced perceptions of powerlessness. Feeling incapable of addressing serious work problems can result in loss of any sense of hope as well as control, and reinforce a fatalistic outlook, both towards the workplace and mental illness itself.

Turning to middle grade civil servants, a lack of control for some individuals was associated with, for example:

- Having too many bosses, too many different and separate items of work.
- Not having the specific skills needed for the task.
- Controlling and overly critical line managers, or few opportunities to discuss work with them.
- Poor communications, such as not being furnished with necessary background information when representing the department at an inter-departmental meeting.
- Workplace changes, such as those involving a sense of loss of ownership of the job.
- Feeling threatened when established work patterns and rules are changed.
- A sense of organisational injustice, feeling powerless to improve chances of promotion for example.
- A determined reliance on self, an expressed need for control, and blaming oneself for not controlling a situation properly when things went wrong.

Some interesting examples were noted in which middle grades reported ways in which they felt able to take control of work issues. Co-operation amongst colleagues, religious faith, and taking a rational approach for example were mentioned in this respect. In some contexts, and in particular work groups, co-operation between colleagues for example, was viewed as essential for rectifying problems. Co-operative social relations are also seen as empowering vis-à-vis management; a collective sense of agency could be strengthened by a departmental culture which encourages participation in decision-making, while individual participants felt empowered. Instances of a rational approach taken towards difficulties mentioned by respondents included refusing to take work problems home or bring home problems to work, a tactic also mentioned by lower grade staff. References to religion featured quite frequently in interviews with this middle grade group. A belief in God and 'taking each day as it comes' helped some to feel in control of their lives.

Higher grade individuals generally report feeling in control at work overall, the degree of decision latitude, for example, was confirmed as grade related. An aspect of their work which they view as incredibly positive is that they can exercise considerable choice, not only in the sense that they decide on what to prioritise but are able to pick up on matters which particularly interest them, or which they enjoy doing. Feeling in control is found satisfying. Some consider control in a wider sense, recognising a combination of factors to be in place for them to feel in control overall. For one, this meant: 'In my own experience feeling in control involves a proper balance between work and home and a reasonably good environment in both, and supportive in both'.

Whilst problems around control issues tend to be less dominant a feature of the work of higher grade civil servants compared to lower and middle grade colleagues, a convergence of negative experiences occurring simultaneously can nevertheless lead to feelings of lack of control even for well-resourced individuals. A man who went through a time when he experienced stress in most aspects of his life felt completely out of control and became seriously depressed. Officials identified specific circumstances at work under which they felt less in control than they wished. Workplace changes in the structure of decision-making were mentioned for example, as were changes in internal politics, matters such as competitive roles in relations with other groups. Some reported feeling out of control in situations where the demands made were external for example, where their usual decision-making capacity had been temporarily removed and certain work had to be prioritised because of ministerial or departmental instructions.

The high volume of work identified by almost all of those interviewed in the Higher Grade group as a source of stress was often mentioned alongside perceptions of diminishing control. Examples included: having to do things at a faster pace than feeling happy with; experiencing conflicting demands such as having to meet deadlines yet wanting to meet one's own expectations on quality; getting through more than feeling capable of doing. The obligation to take on more work for example, together with a lack of staffing to delegate to or of supportive direction from senior management, could leave people feeling especially out of control. Excessive work combined with low control/decision latitude was confirmed as especially stressful across grades. Critically, the damaging effects of experiencing high demands plus low control on mental health and well-being can be exacerbated when certain *meanings* of work, and in particular the value individuals assign to certain bodies of work, are considered. Along with additional and unwelcome demands, when structural changes or promotion take higher grade civil servants away from or impede what they perceive as *valuable* work, the result can be frustration or anxiety and for some, perceptions of diminishing control. It is the onus on them to switch to something which they consider trivial which can make them feel especially devoid of control.

While perceptions of control were important to people across grades, higher grades in the study were more likely than other colleagues to express or achieve a powerful sense of being in control. Along with fewer stressors in life in general and the availability of adequate material and other resources to help them to cope with difficulties, reasons for their favourable position emerging from interviews included, for example, the characteristics and responsibilities of the job at their level, a strong sense of agency and feelings of confidence and optimism. The clear sense of agency common amongst this grade group is evidenced by willingness on their part to *take* control of demanding situations. Examples include an informal support group for part timers who took their problems to management together; a group who took out a collective grievance concerning appraisal reports, and a person wrongly accused in the press of damaging an initiative who coped actively with the situation by writing individually to everyone who had contacted her to explain her actions. A striking feature of civil servants in this grade group concerned the effort they put into managing a wide circle of contacts; they used their well-informed, well-resourced social networks to help them to perform their work effectively and lessen any risk of losing control of it. Amongst Fast Stream officials especially we noticed a continuity of confidence and optimism, nurtured earlier by private schools and Oxbridge and by success in getting through stringent Civil Service recruitment procedures. Perhaps reflecting a conviction of ideas concerning meritocracy, they put effort into their endeavours and expect it to pay dividends. Bridging social capital has been shown to have a stronger effect on mental health than bonding social capital (Pedersen et al., 2023). Bonding social capital may involve social contacts that are similar in type with less access to potentially useful resources.

Coinciding Stressors

Across grades, the study highlights the especially detrimental effects on well-being and mental health of coexisting stressors involving work and/ or home environments. A heavy workload is frequently a key component. Individuals' accounts of their experience of multiple worries and difficulties focused, for example, on feeling overwhelmed together with strong perceptions of losing control. A particular environment at work or outside however, can ameliorate negative effects, through providing support for example, buffering problems or cushioning the individual against them. People in lower grades experiencing multiple problems included a few a-typical examples able to address them effectively with multiple forms of help. These included informal meetings of workmates providing mutual assistance, family support, help from friends, partners or outside agencies, and counselling. For many in this group however, the range of features mitigating negative experience appeared much more restricted. Examples of coinciding stressors experienced by lower grades included cases where new tasks and an added workload were combined with disruption of routines *and* disruption of the social organisation of the unit—such as in cases where shifts were changed or departments re-organised—consequent feelings of loss of control and ensuing psychological distress appeared almost inevitable. Even those higher grades with posts in the upper ranks of their grade group are not always immune from the effects of multiple difficulties. When an episode of high pressure at work is combined with high pressure at home, or when a proper balance could no longer be achieved between work and home, for example, the situation becomes one which could precipitate bouts of anxiety and depression for certain individuals.

Yet our analysis, on the surface, leads us to suspect that there may be a sliding social scale whereby coexisting stressful problems lead to poor well-being and mental ill health. For better advantaged and resourced individuals—as well as material resources this will include positive aspects of work and high levels of satisfaction as well as supports and other effective coping strategies available or adopted—there would need to be a greater number of stressors operating simultaneously for the experience of negative effects than for a person with lower coping or direct resources. The latter we might expect to succumb at a lower level of co-incidence. Overall, our analysis indicates that coping resources tend to increase with grade level; something which needs to be considered when seeking to understand the SEP gradient in depression and well-being. Nevertheless, we can expect the *meanings* invested in both stressors/difficulties and resources/advantages for individuals to play a significant role here, also in the severity of their impact or strength of their effectiveness. Strong meanings, the significance attached to features such as negatively experienced work characteristics, increase the individual's vulnerability and their negative impact; strong meanings relating to positive and satisfying aspects of work or life outside in the home, neighbourhood, or through involvement elsewhere, heighten their efficacy, whether directly to the quality of life and a buffer against stress, or as coping strategies for particular problems. Living in a neighbourhood with a culture of reciprocity or participation, or getting involved in local activities, for example, were important for those who derive happiness from a sense of belonging.

Meanings

Across grades, certain work characteristics, such as a lack of promotion, were found to carry different meanings for different individuals. Some were quite content with their position in the hierarchy for example, this was especially the case for some on lower and middle grades, for whom enjoyable social relations at work and social support, or, in the case of women especially, part time work to suit their family commitments, were perceived as of more value than the advancement of their careers. Others adopted various coping mechanisms to compensate for stalled careers, they included lower grade individuals who were able to interpret their role as high status when compared to their peers outside the Civil Service, and secretaries fulfilling a need for status by identifying with their high-grade boss. But where gaining promotion was highly important to, and expected by individuals, its lack was very keenly felt and a major source of dissatisfaction, perceptions of organisational injustice, and psychological distress.

Examples were noted where meanings and understandings attached to those positive aspects of work considered essential or rewarding could alleviate or shield civil servants against stress. For example, where informal social distractions were appreciated, these could offset boredom amongst lower grades. For some on middle grades and lower rungs of higher grades, problems and difficulties at work passed them by where, for example, they were able to pursue a creative role, or focus on the professional content of their job, activities to which they were highly committed and from which they derive a keen sense of achievement. A higher grade man was able to ignore problems associated with a difficult boss by immersing himself in his work, the content of which he found highly rewarding. Various emotional meanings invested in work, and their derivation, emerged as particularly strong influences on the extent to which characteristics of work generally perceived negatively, such as overwork, lack of promotion, or dull and routine work are considered a problem and reported as stressful. A heavy workload for example was not a problem for a lower grade woman if her work was appreciated, while middle grade civil servants were able to cope with extra demands made on them at the time of an international crisis because they recognised their new work as purposeful, and as highly essential. They were very much committed to it.

Our findings concur, to some extent, with Gaillie et al.'s (2017) suggestion that research should pay more attention to job status anxiety, generated when valued features of the job are at risk. In the present study, when highly appreciated and satisfying aspects of a job—such as good social relations, or the value assigned to particular bodies of work—are threatened, especially damaging health effects can be expected. Consideration of meanings helps widen our understanding of the role of psychosocial pathways such as confidence, esteem, and perceptions of control and organisational injustice in relationships between stressful experience and mental health and well-being. For example, the unwelcome effects of experiencing high demands plus low control on mental health and well-being can be exaggerated when the value individuals assign to particular aspects of work, or its product is compromised. A lower grade woman suffering from depression when interviewed had little interest in returning to her work as what she used to enjoy about the job—the friendliness and sociability of her workmates, and 'knowing what was going on'—no longer existed following departmental staff changes. A lower grade man experiencing anxiety who had changed his job along with its location, very much missed the 'good load of blokes' he used to value working with. For some on higher and middle grades, having to give priority to something which they consider of little intrinsic value, and which was diverting energies from what they perceived as highly important work, resulted in frustration or anxiety alongside diminishing perceptions of control. A higher grade man who had been immensely proud of the achievements of his department and of the quality of what they produced along with its good international reputation found the experience of reorganisation especially distressing as the end result was compromised: 'You have to believe in the value of what you are doing' he insisted. Similarly, a grade three official who had recently left the Civil Service to move into the private sector found his new job less taxing, but nevertheless demoralising and stressful because he saw little value in it, something which for him was an essential requisite for a good and satisfying job.

Especially strong meanings like these can be understood as personal orientations, attitudes and beliefs such as the primacy of social relations across different domains of people's lives, or a paramount need for status, for control, or for finding value in the work undertaken. Additionally, orientations embrace perceptions of the overall significance to the individual of life at work or in the home, in the neighbourhood, or engagement in voluntary activity. For some (mainly) lower grades taking part in the study for example, the main focus of their lives lay outside work altogether, their affective needs—such as those for happiness, contentment, companionship, enjoyment, prestige, or spiritual strength—are met outside work through family, neighbourhood, or social, religious, and other activity. The importance to our well-being of being able to form commitments has been stressed elsewhere (Sayer, 2009). The present study suggests that the depth of the value placed in life outside work increases the efficacy of its potential buffering effect for negatively experienced work characteristics. The example of the man highlighted in Chap. 2, whose strong commitment to several different arenas of his life outside the office appeared able to help prevent him from falling into a state of utter despair at a time when his many work problems were making him very unhappy, is especially pertinent here.

Looked at from a slightly different angle, circumstances under which a work problem becomes stressful, and when not, can be affected also by whether work related and other needs are being met. For example, when interviewees identify factors which make for an ideal job, and these coincide with their experience, then positive effects on well-being can be expected; where they do not, then a stressful outcome related to a particular problem is more likely. Similarly, local neighbourhood life is especially beneficial where people's experiences have affinity with what their needs are, whether these are for peace and quiet for someone who grew up in a noisy household, or for community spirit and neighbourliness for people who, usually, had experienced these as children, or for the centrality of a happy family life for someone whose own childhood had been unhappy and isolating, and so on. Work-based instances include the case of a lower grade man who always felt unsuited to his job in the Civil Service because it did not meet his desire for independence and a sense of achievement, or for control over what he was doing. Consequently, he viewed most aspects of his job negatively and was not able to overcome a long-term inferiority complex.

Social Ties, Networks, and Support: Their Meanings and Structures

Findlay and Thompson (2017) note that negative impacts of change do not affect all workers, or affect them in the same way. Work relationships can help navigate stress for example (Birmingham et al., 2024). For the present study, vital factors moderating negative experience and mental health or well-being include social support available. Social networks—made up of colleagues, friends, family, and others—were confirmed as a positive resource and important source of practical and emotional support. For example, while change and coping with change were common themes across different aspects of the research findings, the part played by the relative stability of the work group was a prominent coping feature. A middle grade man for example, reported that although a downsizing exercise had created a bad feeling amongst departmental staff generally, a combination of an approachable boss, nice colleagues, co-operative working relations, and a sociable work group appeared to enable his own section (a small work group) to handle potentially stressful conditions. Others in this grade group were able to withstand the stress associated with a large number of changes to their jobs essentially because the social organisation peculiar to the team—co-operative work practices and the stability needed to ensure them—went unchanged. Their experience emphasises the strength and importance of peer co-operation at work and trusting relationships when other forms of assistance are no longer available. In contrast, where new tasks and an added workload are combined with disruption of routines *and* disruption of the social organisation of the unit, consequent health problems, as a lower grade woman's account of her experience explained, appeared almost inevitable. She was moved from building to building and was unfamiliar with the working practices of the different locations and with the staff working there. There were further disruptions to the stability of the work group when shifts underwent repeated changes. A context in which it had become impossible for people to support each other contributed to her subsequent depression. The case has relevance for Sennett's (1998) argument that we need to re-establish the dignity of workers. Sennett (2013) has also suggested the co-operation among lower grade employees can be eroded by too much change where time honoured ways of problem-solving are lost, and co-operation is undermined by stress and insecurity enforcing a tendency to self-isolation. In this way the strength of collective efficacy may be weakened.

Quantitative Whitehall II studies have found social support to be highly important for mental health, but do not capture the texture of the support or wider ramifications. These studies found that, while low social support was connected to psychological distress, social support was not a powerful explanation for grade differences in depression (Stansfeld et al., 1999). A probable explanation offered concerned lack of variation between grades in support available. Our analysis of qualitative data suggests however the possibility of other processes occurring, that numbers of supportive ties are not the only criterion to address for example. Thus, if a civil servant on a lower grade were to report similar levels of support to an individual on a higher grade, we could put forward three possible and linked explanations for ensuing processes, all of which take us beyond what can be derived from quantitative work on the subject:

Firstly, the meaning of ties to the individual can be significant and showed some variation between grades. Good social relations at work, being integrated into a co-operative work group for example, are highly valued and make an especially important contribution to both job satisfaction and well-being for people in lower and middle grades, the former especially. Support in this context involves emotional support which provides empathy, belonging, and companionship and boosts self-esteem (Thoits, 2011). It also includes practical support and active coping assistance which may be more relevant in the lower grades (Thoits, 2011; Gariépy et al., 2016). Both emotional and practical support may buffer the impact of stressors at work and at home and prevent the development of depression (Brown & Harris, 1978). Moreover lower social support predicts poorer outcomes from depression (Wang et al., 2018) meaning that low social support at work may prolong existing depression.

For many, the primacy of social relations for lower grades is something which encompasses most spheres of their lives, and their perceptions of well-being. They attach a high value to good social relations in the workplace and local neighbourhood for meeting needs for happiness, contentment, companionship, and enjoyment as well as providing social support. Though social ties were certainly not unimportant to them, those in higher grades tend to emphasise the relevance of other work-related characteristics, such as the value of the work itself, or the degree of self-determination the job facilitates, in contributing to their job satisfaction. Whilst some people in lower grades can gain feelings of empowerment for instance from making demands co-operatively, higher grades can also derive benefits like perceptions of control more directly from the work itself or their position in the hierarchy.

A second possible explanation lies in the structure and resourcefulness of individuals' social networks. Research has emphasised the importance of structurally mixed ties for accessing a wider range of resources, including, as well as emotional or practical support, information on jobs, health care, services, voluntary opportunities, and so on (Cattell, 2001, 2012; Huang & Western, 2011; Song, 2011), while it has been demonstrated that social capital, in the form of access to resources of network members, is negatively associated with the incidence of common mental disorders and psychological distress (Song, 2011; Webber & Huxley, 2007). This has been found particularly for individual cognitive social capital rather than ecological level social capital (De Silva et al., 2005). Earlier work, using narrative accounts of the everyday lives of residents in low-income neighbourhoods, highlighted the significance of different network patterns for mediating disadvantage and experience of health, well-being, and happiness. It found that those with heterogeneous network structures were in an advantaged position when compared with those whose networks, even if numerically extensive, were narrower in scope. Extensive social ties made up of family members and neighbours for example were usually very effective in providing practical support, but could nevertheless be limited in providing coping resources for a wider array of needs for example (Cattell, 2003; Cattell, 2012). Taking a different view, Cornwell and Laumann (2015) suggest that people with broader networks will be exposed to a wider range of stimuli than those with more homogenous ties.

Qualitative data derived from our present study presented an opportunity to look at some of the issues noted above across different socio-economic groups. It has been suggested that we need to look at social class in dynamic ways, attuned to the complexity of social networks for example (Savage et al., 2013; Savage, 2015). Like many resources, access to productive and resourceful social networks varies across social groups (Pearlin, 1985); the networks of higher grade individuals in the present study were generally found to be differentially structured and highly resourced. There were examples of officials actively managing looser, wider ties, made through their Oxbridge College for example, to garner expert information and advice to help them with work-related matters and problems. While the educational level of members of an individual's network has been shown in itself to be positively associated with that individual's life satisfaction and linked negatively to anomie (Acock &

Hurlbert, 1993), privileged individuals, such as these Civil Service fast streamers, are able to draw on another level of prestige and power through diverse membership groups and social networks embodying a high degree of social and cultural capital.

A third aspect of our exploration into why social support in the Whitehall II studies was not a powerful explanation for grade differences in depression, is connected not only to the high esteem placed on features like good social relations and support voiced by lower grade staff, but also to their very reliance on them. We suggest that this feature is also connected to lower grades having fewer additional resources at their disposal than middle and higher grade colleagues. While an earlier study (Cattell, 2001, 2012) suggested that social network models were an expression of the richness and impoverishment of lives lived, the present study uncovers additional linked factors.

Richer or More Restricted Lives

Processes we've described illustrating vulnerability and resilience help contribute to explanations focussing on the employment grade or social class gradient in depression. Quantitative Whitehall II studies have demonstrated that lower grades have a higher risk of depression and that the impact of exposure to negative work characteristics on mental health is worse for lower grades (Stansfeld et al., 2003). This book indicates that lower grades may not only experience many sources of dissatisfaction, but that avenues available for civil servants to cope with, remedy, or offset a problem become apparently fewer with decreasing grade. The range of sources of satisfaction—a key mediator—available to lower grades for example was narrower for them than for their more senior colleagues in middle and higher grades. Lower grades taking part in the study gain little satisfaction from the actual job tasks themselves for instance. Some people can be quite content to lead relatively limited lives, enjoying good social relations with colleagues perhaps, or a happy family life, but when things go awry, or a crisis occurs, these individuals have less to fall back on than more advantaged colleagues, and can be in a poorer position to avoid feeling overwhelmed and out of control. An added problem with reliance on good social ties at work or at home can be their very fragility. For example, lower grades in certain contexts are not only likely to experience more disruptions to the work group but staffing changes (involving dislocation of supports) are also likely to have a greater detrimental impact upon them than on their more senior colleagues. In part this is because their work-based ties are invested with especially positive value, but also because we could expect greater negative effects on people for whom other resources, such as sources of satisfaction, are limited. An interesting example of relations between support and co-operation and additional resources concerns the experience of a middle grade man whose work group had lost many of the work-based resources previously at their disposal and which had assisted them in carrying out their work—features such as libraries, training, and technical assistance—and so had been forced to rely heavily on each other instead to resolve difficulties.

Overall, fewer factors mitigating or ameliorating stressful experience inside or outside the workplace means less cushioning, buffering, or remedying of the problem; restricted diversity in support available; less chance of needs being met; and a greater risk of poor mental health. Conversely, we noted a strong tendency for variety of experience, for opportunities to live richer lives or simply to get more out of life, to broaden with increasing grade. Middle, like their lower grade colleagues, express dissatisfaction with their jobs, but a wider range of factors mitigating negative experience were apparent amongst the former. Satisfaction derived from the content of the job itself was mentioned by middle grades participating in the study, and almost universally amongst people in higher grades. For some in the professional statistical or creative stratum for example, the professional content of the job, or its creative aspects, are sources of pride, enjoyment, and achievement. Wide sources of satisfaction and pleasure both within and outside of the workplace strengthen the individual's ability to cope with dissatisfactions and problems by widening and diversifying sources of support for example as noted, but also by cushioning individuals against adverse experience, or acting as buffer or distraction from a particular problem.

The nineteenth-century writer William Morris believed that it is the very variety of life which is pivotal to our happiness and well-being (Morris, 1974). Higher grades in our study gain a great deal of gratification from many aspects of their work: its content, its challenging aspects, its valued contribution to the common good, amongst them. Satisfying work can act to cushion or compensate for home and other problems or buffer their negative impacts. These kinds of benefits are not restricted to the higher grades, but clearly, we could expect the higher the job satisfaction for an individual for example, the more effective the buffer. By contrast some middle grades, or higher grades at the slightly lower end of their grade group, were enjoying a balanced life, in the sense of being able to pursue outside interests such as music, hobbies, or participating in voluntary work, activities which were able to help mitigate work pressures as well as being of direct benefit to well-being.

A richer life experience will also provide more opportunities for an individual's needs to be met. This is evident in the workplace for example, where higher grades recognise a wide range of positive factors necessary to co-exist for meaningful job satisfaction to be realised, most of which they have, and critically for them, include the need to find value in the work they do. Higher grades are better placed to experience what they want from a job; few will end up as 'square pegs in round holes', a phrase used by a lower grade man to describe his perception of his own job. More generally, people whose needs were being met in several major domains of their lives were particularly fortunate. Individuals undertaking voluntary work, for example, were in an especially strong position to lead a full and balanced life, and through this achieve what they desire. An ability to balance work and non-work has been ranked highly for job satisfaction elsewhere (Findlay & Thompson, 2017). Of particular interest in the present study, were those civil servants, generally in middle grades and lower levels of higher grades, able to realise their ambition to help and improve the lives of others, to contribute to the common good, for their endeavours and the product of their work to have value, and to gain a sense of achievement and develop commitment, both at work *and* through volunteering outside the workplace. As well as deriving therapeutic benefit from valued activities targeted at helping others, a conviction to lead a balanced life—and achieving it—made for a richer and happier life.

Advantage and Disadvantage

While we have demonstrated that meanings attached to a wide range of positive and negative experiences have a significant role to play in processes affecting individual well-being and mental health, we have nonetheless considered them within a context of advantage or disadvantage. An apparent grade gradient in sources of satisfaction already discussed does not mean that material advantages should be side-lined. For example, people whose needs were being met in several major areas of their lives were more likely to be those with a good or adequate income, broadening their choice of action, and protecting against the damaging effects of unexpected financial difficulties, while owning a second home in attractive surrounding made it easier for higher grades to cope with the nuisance value of taking work home at weekends. For those on low incomes, an unexpected financial difficulty can trigger depression in persons already experiencing multiple stressors. Stability of residence—a prime source of social capital—and its implications for developing and sustaining local social ties and involvement, though also experienced by people in lower grades living in decent quality social housing for instance, appeared most common amongst those in higher grades who had been able to buy good sized properties in very pleasant locations relatively early in their careers. At the same time, where local ties are important to one's life, and are dislocated by divorce, moving, or local change, their loss can be keenly felt by people across the grade spectrum. Those higher up the grade scale however can be in a better position than others to improve their situation, by moving into a pleasant area with plentiful opportunities for local engagement for example, whereas disrupted ties are more difficult to rectify for those with low incomes living in an area of economic decline and out migration.

No less important than income here are education and a privileged background: higher education has been found to offer some protection to age related depression for example (Miech & Shanahan, 2000). In our study, benefits derived from the capacity for applying rational thought in the contributions of those taking part, appeared to a certain extent grade related. A rational approach when encountering and coping with unreasonable work demands displayed by some professionally qualified middle grades who neither totally blamed themselves or the system for difficulties, for example, was considered by them to be protective. For some of our higher grade civil servants, attendance at an elite university, and the confidence, opportunities, achievements, and assurances it brings, as well as highly resourced social networks, can also encompass potential benefits to mental health and well-being. Higher grades display a stronger sense of agency compared to some lower and middle grades for example when addressing and coping with problems.

Occupations have taken a pivotal role in the analysis of social class (Harrison & Scott, 2020) and of social inequalities in health—an assumption which is questioned from time to time. For ethical socialists such as Tawney, the British class system was based not only on the inequitable distribution of wealth and other material resources, but of power, privilege, culture, and opportunity too (Tawney, 1931). Class distinctions find new ways of expressing themselves (Hoggett, 2001). Recent developments in approaches to class theory are of particular interest when looking at the employment grade gradient in mental health and well-being addressed here. Following Pierre Bourdieu (1986), who sought sources of capitals, Savage and Devine and their colleagues measure class with reference to the different kinds of economic, cultural, and social resources—capitals—people possess (Savage et al., 2013; Savage et al., 2014; Savage, 2015). They hope their model might cross fertilise with qualitative research to produce a more developed multi-dimensional approach. Our research did not set out to examine innovative approaches to categorising SEP, but our analyses of interview data do help illustrate some of the dimensions of class groupings utilised by their schema and draw attention to the all-pervasive nature of class evident in many aspects of our lives. Unlike Savage and his colleagues, we began with grade groupings (an approximate proxy for SEP) however; but as analysis progressed, were able to identify some aspects of social and cultural capital associated with these groupings. While these writers referred to conceive of their seven classes as the *product* of the interplay of the three different capitals which comprise them, we might suggest that relationships between SEP on the one hand, and resources and advantages—including economic, social, and cultural capital—might usefully be considered as recursive.

Quality Work

We have witnessed a growth nationally in work-related stress, depression, and anxiety since 2010, and an increase in poor quality work, as measured by factors such as insecure jobs (Marmot et al., 2020). Recent studies looking at 'good work' have focused on components of 'quality work' (see, e.g., Taylor, 2017). For the Work Foundation for example, this embraces such features as employment security; work that is not characterised by monotony and repetition; autonomy, control, and task discretion; a balance between the efforts workers make and the rewards they receive; whether the workers have the skills they need to cope with periods of intense pressure; observance of the basic principles of procedural justice; and strong workplace relationships (Coates & Lekhi, 2008). The present study, which has included a focus on those things which people find satisfying, fulfilling, or beneficial, or, by their absence, dissatisfying and damaging to mental health and well-being, can concur with these positive aspects of work itemised by the Work Foundation. We have highlighted features of good and poor quality work additional to those they suggest however, these include the benefits of co-operative relations, and the negative impact of a lack of promotion, inadequate support during periods of change, as well as overwork and coinciding stressors. An important finding in relation to quality work as understood by civil servants participating in our study concerns the degree of value individuals see in the work undertaken, in work that is meaningful, work that is a public good, with potential to improve the lives of others, and to which they are committed. Yet a YouGov (2015) poll has found that 37% of British workers did not believe that their job made a meaningful contribution to the world, while engaging in work believed to be pointless is judged as psychologically destructive (Graeber, 2018). Mathew Taylor (2021), an advocate of good work, suggests the adoption of 'Good Work for All' as a rallying cry. Perhaps however, as Findlay and Thompson (2017) suggest, we need a more nuanced understanding of positive elements of 'bad' jobs, and more negative elements of 'good' ones. The present study shows nonetheless that positive or negatively experienced job characteristics are influenced in no small part by the meanings and value held by individuals and grade groups.

In society at large, inequalities in the availability of good, enjoyable work generally have been referred to elsewhere as 'contributory injustice' something which limits the extent to which people can develop their own abilities and find fulfilment (Cieslik, 2015; Gomberg, 2007). This book emphasises that satisfying features of work in general, and work that is meaningful, valued, purposeful, and which attracts commitment, is not evenly distributed across employment grades in the study. The higher the grade of the individual civil servant, the more value they were likely to attribute to the work which they did and to recognise many positive features of their job. A focus on meanings and value of work contributes to our understanding of social inequalities in mental health and well-being and nudges us towards exploring possible means of helping to rectify them.

In summation, the findings of earlier Whitehall II quantitative study research which showed that social support does not explain the grade gradient in depression can be better understood, we suggest, with reference to grade variation in: (a) the meaning of social relations and support, and their value; (b) the structure of social ties and their enabling access to resources; and (c) the additional resources and positive features of work and life outside available to individuals. The role of sources of job satisfaction, for example, in alleviating or buffering stressful experience is significant. The same features have relevance to earlier quantitative Whitehall studies which demonstrated that lower grades are affected more by negative work characteristics than are their higher grade colleagues. Other than social support, we found fewer additional resources available to lower grades to help them cope with or overcome the problems they encountered.

Yet our findings suggest complexity in relation to processes involved. Not only are a wide range of resources and advantages available to higher grades, but higher grade individuals reported that certain positive work characteristics were needed to co-exist alongside others for them to be especially effective. Civil servants in the same grade group also recognise the need for a combination of positive factors to be in place for them to feel in control overall. An apparent cumulative effect helps to explain why lower grades are more affected by negative work characteristics than are their more advantaged colleagues. Health inequalities can be seen here to be self-perpetuating, as was the tendency noted earlier that perceptions of lack of control have increasing significance at different stages of the stress process, a pattern which had especial relevance to the experience of lower grade civil servants.

Policy Implications

Employers across sectors should be encouraged to invest in the mental health of their staff. Introducing mental health practitioners or mental health first aiders into the workplace are amongst measures starting to be adopted and which are likely to be beneficial for example. Our research suggests that employers generally could usefully find ways to take account of workplace characteristics which are important to people, in both a positive and negative sense. This could be undertaken during the annual performance review perhaps. To reduce gaps between grades concerning opportunities available to lead lives associated with positive well-being, renewed effort needs to be put into understanding differing sources of job satisfaction and dissatisfaction found in diverse levels of seniority. Nonetheless, across the board problems such as the intense and excessive work schedule described by some civil servants or the long hours culture identified by others are simply not tenable for achieving a balanced life or good mental health. This is not just a problem for families when the children are young, but as our middle-aged cohort indicated, can be an issue at any point during working lives. A shortened working week is likely to be highly beneficial. Rather than, through inaction, laying themselves open to accusations of 'social murder', to use Engels's (1844) term, measures taken by employers or policy makers to address the various issues explored and highlighted in this study will have implications for grade related health inequalities as well as for improvements to mental health and well-being more generally.

References

Acock, A. C., & Hurlbert, J. S. (1993). Social Networks, Marital Status, and Well-being. *Social Networks, 15*(3), 309–334.

Birmingham, W. C., et al. (2024). 'The Positive Side of Social Connections in the Workplace. *American Journal of Health Promotion, 38*(6), 886–891.

Bourdieu, P. (1986). The Forms of Capital. Pp. 241-258 in Handbook of Theory and Research for the Sociology of Education, edited by J. G. Richardson. Greenwood Press.

Brown, G. W., & Harris, T. (1978). *Social Origins of Depression*. Tavistock.

Cattell, V. (2001). Poor People, Poor Places, and Poor Health: The Mediating Role of Social Networks and Social Capital. *Social Science and Medicine, 52*(10), 1501–1516.

Cattell, V. (2003). Social Networks as Mediators Between the Harsh Circumstances of People's Lives and Their Lived Experience of Health and Well-being. In C. Phillipson, G. Allan, & D. Morgan (Eds.), *Social Networks and Social Exclusion: Sociological and Policy Perspectives* (pp. 142–161). Ashgate.

Cattell, V. (2012). *Poverty, Community and Health: Co-operation and the Good Society*. Palgrave Macmillan.

Cieslik, M. (2015). Sociology and the Problem of Happiness. *Sociology, 49*(3), 422–437.

Coates, D. with Lekhi, R. (2008). *Good Work: Job Quality in a Changing Economy*. The Work Foundation.

Cornwell, B., & Laumann, E. O. (2015). The Health Benefits of Network Growth: New Evidence from a National Survey of Older Adults. *Social Science and Medicine, 125*, 94–98.

De Silva, M. J., McKenzie, K., Harpham, T., & Huttly, S. R. A. (2005). Social Capital and Mental Illness: A Systematic Review. *Journal of Epidemiology and Community Health, 9*(8), 619–627.

Engels, F. (1844). *The Condition of the Working Class in England*. Penguin Books.

Findlay, P., & Thompson, P. (2017). Contemporary Work; Its Meanings and Demands. *Journal of Industrial Relations, 59*(2), 122–138.

Gaillie, D., Felstead, A., Green, F., & Inanc, H. (2017). The Hidden Face of Job Insecurity. *Work, Employment and Society, 31*(1), 36–53.

Gariépy, G., Honkaniemi, H., & Quesnel-Vallée, A. (2016). Social Support and Protection from Depression: Systematic Review of Current Findings in Western Countries. *British Journal of Psychiatry, 209*(4), 284–293.

Gomberg, P. (2007). *How to Make Opportunity Equal: Race and Contributory Justice*. Wiley.
Graeber, D. (2018). *Bullshit Jobs: The Rise of Pointless Work, and What We Can Do About It*. Simon and Schuster.
Harrison, E. and Scott, J. (2020). Class and Stratification in G. Payne and E. Harrison (eds.) Social Divisions, Class and Inequality in Britain, Policy Press.
Hoggett, P. (2001). *Agency, Rationality and Social Policy*. Cambridge University Press, Cambridge.
Huang, X., & Western, M. (2011). Social Networks and Occupational Attainment in Australia. *Sociology, 45*(2), 269–286.
Kawachi, I., Subramanian, S. V., & Kim, D. (2010). *Social Capital and Health*. Springer.
Malik, O. F., et al. (2021). Workplace Psychological Aggression, Job Stress, and Vigor: A Test of Longitudinal Effects. *Journal of Interpersonal Violence, 36*(5-6), Np3222-3240.
Marmot, S. M., et al. (2020). *Health Equity in England: The Marmot Review 10 Years on*. UCL Institute of Health Equity.
Miech, R. A., & Shanahan, J. (2000). Socioeconomic Status and Depression over the Life Course. *Journal of Health and Social Behaviour, 41*(2), 162–176.
Morris, W. (1974). In J. Redmond (Ed.), *News from Nowhere*. Routlege.
Pearlin, L. I. (1985). Social structure and processes of social support. In S. Cohen & S. L. Syme (Eds.), Social support and health (pp. 43–60). Academic Press.
Pedersen, L. M., Laursen, S., & Buttenschøn, H. N. (2023). Is Mental Health Positively Associated with Workplace Social Capital among Danish Hospital Employees? A multilevel Study. *Mental Health & Prevention, 32*(5), 200300.
Putnam, R. D. (2000). *Bowling Alone: The Collapse and Revival of American Community*. Simon and Schuster.
Savage, M., Devine, F., & Miles, A. (2013). A New Model of Social Class. *Sociology, 47*(2), 219–250.
Savage, M., Devine, F., & Taylor, M. (2014). On Social Class, Anno 2014. *Sociology, 49*(6), 1011–1030.
Savage, M. (2015). *Social Class in the 21st Century*. Pelican.
Sayer, A. (2009). Contributive justice and meaningful work'. *Res Publica 15*(1), 1–6.
Sennett, R. (1998). *Corrosion of character: the personal consequences of work in the new capitalism*. W. W. Norton and Co.
Sennett, R. (2013). *Together: The Rituals, Pleasures & Politics of Cooperation*. Penguin Books.
Song, L. (2011). Social Capital and Psychological Distress. *Journal of Health and Psychological Distress, 52*(4), 478–492.
Stansfeld, S. A., Head, J., & Marmot, M. G. (1999). Explaining Social Class Differences in Depression and Well-being. *Social Psychiatry and Psychiatric Epidemiology, 33*, 1–9.

Stansfeld, S. A., & Candy, B. (2006). Psychosocial Work Environment and Mental Health - a Meta-analytical Review. *Scandinavian Journal of Work Environment and Health, 32*(6), 443–462.
Stansfeld, S. A., Head, J., Fuhrer, R., Wardle, J., & Cattell, V. (2003) Social Inequalities in Depressive Symptoms and Physical Functioning in the Whitehall II Study: Exploring a Common Cause Explanation. *Journal of Epidemiology and Community Health, 57*(5), 361–367.
Tawney, R. H. (1931/1964). *Equality*. Allen and Unwin.
Taylor, M. (2017). *Good Work: The Taylor Review of Modern Working Practices: A Review Submitted to the UK Government*. Royal Society of Arts.
Taylor, M. (2021). *Do We Have to Work? A Primer for the 21st Century*. Thames and Hudson.
Thoits, P. A. (2011). Mechanisms Linking Social Ties and Support to Physical and Mental Health. *Journal of Health and Social Behavior, 52*(2), 145–161.
Wallston, K. A., Wallston, B. S., Smith, S., & Dobbins, C. J. (1987). Perceived Control and Health. *Current Psychological Health and Reviews, 6*, 5–25.
Wang, J., Mann, F., & Lloyd-Evans, B. et al. (2018). Associations between loneliness and perceived social support and outcomes of mental health problems: A systematic review. *BMC Psychiatry, 18*, 156.
Webber, M. P., & Huxley, P. J. (2007). Measuring Access to Social Capital: The Validity and Reliability of the Resource Generator-UK and Its Association with Common Mental Disorder'. *Social Science and Medicine, 65*(3), 481–492.
YouGov. (2015). *37% Of British Workers Think Their Jobs Are Meaningless*. www.yougov.co.uk

Summary

The role and value of work for the twenty-first century has become a prominent focus of interest. Discussion has focused on both benefits and harmful effects of the working environment. The Whitehall II Stress and Health studies have highlighted inequities and shown the many disbenefits of employment to be unevenly distributed between social groups. Yet we suspected that the quantitative differences identified in these studies may not provide the whole picture: the effects of pathways linking features such as work characteristics and material factors to common mental disorders or to positive aspects of well-being could be expected to be conveyed through the *meaning* of stressors for example, or mediated through individual perceptions of work.

Based on a qualitative research project, this book examines and illustrates ways in which a wide range of stressors, mitigators, and resources are not only socially distributed and experienced but also interpreted and understood by men and women in different civil service grades. Adopting a holistic and sociological approach to the research helps us to understand why some people and not others in given circumstances feel out of control or become anxious or depressed.

Seventy-six in-depth interviews with a sub-sample of middle-aged civil servants were carried out across different employment grades—lower,

V. Cattell, S. Stansfeld, *Work in the Balance*,
https://doi.org/10.1007/978-3-031-96582-1

middle, and higher grades. The interviews were set within the wider framework of respondents' everyday lives.

Lower, Middle, and Higher Grades

Based on rich narratives, our findings demonstrate grade variation as well as commonality in the breadth and kinds of stressors experienced and resources available to people in their working lives and outside paid employment and consider some of the meanings invested in them. Common dissatisfactions and stressors across grades, for example, included work overload, workplace change, negative experience of the annual reporting system (triggering a sense of injustice), and a lack of promotion for those who desired or expected it. The especially deleterious effects on mental health and well-being of a combination of stressors occurring at one time were commonly experienced.

Particular stressors deriving from the workplace can be more common in lower grades: a lack of confidence when performing new tasks without adequate training was experienced as stressful, for example, as were difficult relationships, communication problems, uncertainty about the future, dysfunctional work units, and feeling alienated from the working environment. Lower grade civil servants on the whole did not expect to gain much satisfaction from the actual content of the work, but potential difficulties like performing routine tasks, for example, were not necessarily a problem if they gained enjoyment from other aspects of the job. The most prominent feature of this grade group concerned the primacy of experiencing good social relations and friendly and supportive social ties at work and outside work. Where good working relationships with peers and bosses were disrupted by changes in the social organisation of the department or unit, the workplace could become a source of stress.

Middle grade civil servants were able to pinpoint their enjoyment of specific work tasks. Working structures which encourage teamwork and co-operative working arrangements are appreciated as is an understanding for some that their work is of value, for example. Many dislike change, and some believe that experience is now appreciated less, that the certainty of career progression had gone, and that order and predictability were being eroded. Involvement in outside activities and through this achieving a work-life balance was an especially prominent feature of this middle grade group, something valued highly by respondents and understood by them as beneficial to their psychological health.

Along with experiencing a good standard of living and its benefits in relation to coping with stressful issues, instrumental features which stand out as typical of the experience of higher grades include commitment and dedication to their work, their belief in its value, and contribution to the common good. A powerful sense of agency is driven by strong feelings of confidence, by a belief that they can achieve success, and that problems can be remedied. Expressions of the great deal of satisfaction gained from the work that they do were striking. Work was considered dissatisfying and frustrating; however, control shifted, when governmental directives or departmental initiatives needed to be given priority.

Perceptions of Control

The study confirms earlier work demonstrating perceptions of control as especially important pathways in processes involved in mental health and well-being. Understandings of lack of control commonly expressed by lower and middle grade civil servants were associated with many factors. Examples of particularly acute perceptions of powerlessness amongst lower grades were linked to: (i) an inability to settle a problem because help from senior management or the union was not available and (ii) alienation from the work tasks, the product of the work, and from colleagues. The data suggests that perceptions of lack of control can have increasing significance for people at various stages of the stress process. Firstly, experiencing an objective or structured lack of control at work in a job closely supervised or responding to the needs and instructions of others; secondly, experiencing problems and difficulties; thirdly, having insufficient coping resources, including support, or feeling options blocked; and fourthly, becoming anxious or depressed.

Some interesting examples were noted in which middle grades reported ways in which they felt able to take control of difficult work issues. Co-operation amongst colleagues, religious faith, and taking a rational approach, for example, were mentioned in this respect. Higher grade individuals generally report feeling in control at work overall; the degree of decision latitude, for example, was confirmed as grade related. Whilst problems around control issues tend to be less dominant a feature of the work of higher grade civil servants compared to lower and middle grade colleagues, a convergence of negative experiences occurring simultaneously can nevertheless lead to feelings of lack of control even for well-resourced individuals, while an over heavy workload could act to nullify the positive aspects of the job and have a detrimental impact on their mental health and well-being.

Coinciding Stressors

Across grades, the study highlights the especially detrimental effects on well-being and mental health of coexisting stressors involving work and/or home environments. We suggest that there may be a sliding social scale whereby coexisting stressful problems lead to mental ill health. For better advantaged and resourced individuals—as well as material resources this will include positive aspects of work and high levels of satisfaction, as well as supports and other effective coping strategies available or adopted—there would need to be a greater number of stressors operating simultaneously for the experience of negative effects than for a person with lower coping or direct resources. The latter we might expect to succumb at a lower level of co-incidence. Overall, our analysis indicates that coping resources tend to increase with grade level. Nevertheless, the meanings invested in both stressors/difficulties and resources/advantages for individuals play a significant role here also in the severity of their impact or strength of their effectiveness.

Meanings

Across grades, certain work characteristics, such as a lack of promotion, were found to carry different meanings for different individuals. Some were quite content with their position in the hierarchy, for example, but where gaining promotion was highly important too, and expected, its lack was very keenly felt and a major source of dissatisfaction, perceptions of injustice, and psychological distress.

Examples were noted where meanings and understandings attached to those positive aspects of work considered essential or rewarding could alleviate or shield civil servants against stress. For example, for some on middle grades and lower rungs of higher grades, problems and difficulties at work passed them by where, for example, they were able to pursue a creative role, or focus on the professional content of their job: activities from which they derive a keen sense of achievement. A higher grade man was able to ignore problems associated with a difficult boss by immersing himself in his work, the content of which he found rewarding. Some middle grade civil servants were able to cope with extra demands made on them at a time of international crisis because they considered the work to be essential. When highly appreciated and satisfying aspects of a job are threatened, especially damaging health effects can be expected. 'You have to believe in the value of what you are doing', insisted a higher grade man. Consideration of meanings helps widen our understanding of the role of psychosocial pathways such as confidence, esteem, and perceptions of control in relationships between stressful experience and mental health and well-being.

Especially strong meanings can also be understood as personal orientations, attitudes, and beliefs such as the centrality of social relations across different domains of people's lives, or a paramount need for status, for control, or for finding value in the work undertaken. Additionally, orientations embrace perceptions of the overall significance to the individual of life at work or in the home, in the neighbourhood, or participation in voluntary activity. For some lower grades taking part in the study, for example, the main focus of their lives lay outside work altogether; their affective needs are met outside work through family, neighbourhood, or social, religious, and other activity. The depth of the value placed in life outside work increases the efficacy of its potential buffering effect for negatively experienced work characteristics. The example of the man highlighted in Chap. 2, whose strong commitment to several different arenas of his life appeared able to help prevent him from falling into a state of utter despair at a time when his many work problems were making him very unhappy, is especially pertinent here.

Social Ties and Social Networks

Vital factors moderating negative experience and mental health or well-being include social support available. Social networks—made up of colleagues, friends, family, and others—were confirmed as a generally positive resource. For example, while change and coping with change were common themes across different aspects of the research findings, the part played by the relative stability of the work group was a prominent coping feature. Some middle graders were able to withstand the stress associated with a large number of changes to their jobs essentially because the social organisation peculiar to the team—co-operative work practices and the social stability needed to ensure them—went unchanged. Their experience emphasises the strength and importance of peer co-operation at work and trusting relationships when other forms of assistance—like libraries and technical and managerial support—are no longer available. In contrast, where new tasks and an added workload are combined with disruption of routines *and* disruption of the social organisation of the unit, as experienced by some in lower grades, consequent health problems appeared almost inevitable. A context in which it becomes impossible for people to support each other contributed to subsequent depression.

The findings of an earlier Whitehall II quantitative study which showed that social support does not explain the grade gradient in depression can be better understood, we suggest, with reference to grade variation in: (a) the meaning of social relations and support, and their value; (b) the structure of social ties and their enabling access to resources; and (c) the additional resources and positive features of work and life outside available to individuals. The role of sources of job satisfaction for example in alleviating or buffering stressful experience is significant. Similar features also have relevance to findings of earlier quantitative Whitehall II studies, which demonstrated that lower grades are affected more by negative work characteristics than are their higher grade colleagues. This book not only notes the high esteem placed on features like good social relations and support voiced by lower grade staff, but also their necessary reliance on them. Lower grades have fewer additional resources at their disposal than middle and higher grade colleagues, to help them cope with or overcome the problems they encounter.

Advantage and Disadvantage

Overall, fewer factors mitigating or ameliorating stressful experience inside or outside the workplace mean less cushioning, buffering, or remedying of the problem, restricted diversity in support available, less chance of wants being met, and a greater risk of poor mental health. Conversely, we noted a strong tendency for variety of experience, for getting more out of life, to broaden with increasing grade. Middle, like their lower grade colleagues, express dissatisfactions with their jobs, but a wider range of factors mitigating negative experience were apparent amongst the former. Satisfaction derived from the content of the job itself was mentioned by middle grades participating in the study, and almost universally amongst people in higher grades. Higher grades are better placed to avoid ending up as 'square pegs in round holes'.

An apparent grade gradient in sources of satisfaction discussed does not mean that material advantages should be side-lined. For example, for those on low incomes, an unexpected financial difficulty can trigger depression in persons already experiencing multiple stressors. At the same time, disrupted ties are more difficult to rectify for those with low incomes living in an area of economic decline and out migration.

No less important than income are education and a privileged background. For some higher grade civil servants, attendance at an elite university, and the confidence, opportunities, achievements, and assurances it brings, as well as highly resourced social networks, can also encompass potential benefits to mental health and well-being. Recent developments in class theory are of particular interest when looking at the employment grade gradient in mental health and well-being addressed here. Savage and Devine and their colleagues measure class with reference to the different kinds of economic, cultural, and social resources—capitals—people possess (Savage et al, 2015; 2013). Our analyses of interview data help illustrate some of the dimensions of class groupings they utilise and draw attention to the all-pervasive nature of socio-economic position evident in many aspects of our lives.

Quality Work

We have witnessed a growth nationally in work-related stress, depression, and anxiety since 2010, and an increase in poor quality work. An important finding in relation to quality work as understood by civil servants participating in our study concerns the degree of value individuals see in the work undertaken, in work that is meaningful, work that is a public good, with potential to improve the lives of others, and to which they are committed. Yet a YouGov (2015) poll has found that 37% of British workers did not believe that their job made a meaningful contribution to the world. This book emphasises that satisfying features of work are not evenly distributed across employment grades in the study. Additionally, an apparent cumulative effect concerning positive or negative characteristics of work indicates the self-perpetuating nature of health inequalities.

Policy implication suggested include the need for a shorter working week. Across the board problems such as the intense and excessive work schedule described by some civil servants or the long hours culture identified by others are simply not tenable for achieving a balanced life or good mental health. This is not just a problem for families when the children are young, but as our middle-aged cohort indicated, can be an issue at any point during working lives.

Vicky Cattell
Stephen Stansfeld

Index

V. Cattell, S. Stansfeld, *Work in the Balance*,
https://doi.org/10.1007/978-3-031-96582-1

GPSR Compliance

The European Union's (EU) General Product Safety Regulation (GPSR) is a set of rules that requires consumer products to be safe and our obligations to ensure this.

If you have any concerns about our products, you can contact us on ProductSafety@springernature.com

In case Publisher is established outside the EU, the EU authorized representative is:

Springer Nature Customer Service Center GmbH
Europaplatz 3
69115 Heidelberg, Germany

Batch number: 08832368

Printed by Printforce, the Netherlands